PLANNING HOMES FOR THE AGED

PLANNING

GENEVA MATHIASEN

Executive Secretary,
National Committee on the Aging,
National Social Welfare Assembly

EDWARD H. NOAKES

Edward H. Noakes & Associates,
Architects

Editors

HOMES FOR THE AGED

 F. W. DODGE CORPORATION, NEW YORK

© 1959 by F. W. Dodge Corporation

Printed and bound in U.S.A.

This book or any part thereof must not be reproduced in any form without the written permission of the publisher.

Library of Congress Catalog Card No. 59-8314

Foreword

Many factors indicate a substantial increase in the number of homes for the aged to be built in the future, and some of these factors are also influencing the architectural design of such homes.

The most important spur to this kind of construction is, of course, the population trend (shown in Appendix A). While accurate figures on the number of older people living in institutions are not available, it is estimated that approximately 5 per cent of those over 65 live outside their own homes, the greatest proportion in homes for the aged and nursing homes. With the number of those 65 and over increasing at the rate of about 2,000 a day, an active building program is essential simply to meet current needs.

A second factor is greater availability of funds. Through social security benefits, often augmented by industrial pensions, many older people are now able to pay for better living accommodations and care than formerly—or at least to make a greater contribution toward the cost of this care. At the same time, federal and sometimes state funds have made possible long-term, low-cost loans that ease the financial load of new construction.

A third factor is the state of health of older people. Medical science has eliminated many of the causes of early death, and many more people are reaching the later years in a more vigorous and healthy state than their forebears. The combination of improved health and increased income enables people to live independently much longer than formerly. The average age of residents in institutions has increased about 10 years—to about 80—in the last two decades, and their average age at admission is in the middle seventies.

However, the chronic illnesses for which medical science has as yet found no cure are much more prevalent among this age group than among the rest of the population. For this reason, a home for the aged must provide infirmary care for those who will need it. At the same time, advances in medicine's rehabilitative techniques and the discovery that the greatest possible participation in life is important to the well-being of the elderly, combine to overcome the effects of increased age and produce a more active group of residents. All these factors must be considered by those who plan and build homes for the aged.

Probably the least tangible and yet the most crucial consideration in planning the new buildings is that of making them homes rather than institutions. Board members and others responsible for a home should plan the kind of life that will be most conducive to the maximum health, happiness, and well-being of all residents. The architect must use skill and imagination to provide the physical surroundings within which such a plan can be fulfilled.

So far, there has been very little material in the literature of architecture to serve as a guide to architects and planners of such homes. This book has been prepared to help provide both the philosophical base and the practical criteria required in the planning and building of homes for elderly people.

Eleven contributors, with wide experience in the field, have each written a chapter in Section I of this book. Because of some overlapping of subject matter, the editors have taken certain liberties in combining and rearranging material. Therefore, although the chapters are signed, they are not all in the exact form in which they were submitted.

The illustrations for this book represent some of the entries in a competition for the design of a home for the aged sponsored by the National Committee on the Aging of the National Social Welfare Assembly in conjunction with the magazines *Architectural Record* and *The Modern Hospital*. The six winning designs are shown in Section II with commentary by the contestants, the chairman of the jury, and the architectural editor. A program of the competition is also included. The text of Section I is illustrated by other entries in the competition, with commentary by the architectural editor.

Prizes for the award-winning entries as well as funds for administering the competition and preparing the material for this volume were contributed, through the National Committee on the Aging, by the Schimper Foundation of New York.

The Modern Hospital and *Architectural Record* publicized the competition through their advertising and editorial pages. They also published special articles which, in reprint form, were available to contestants.

The National Committee on the Aging is deeply grateful to the many persons and organizations whose efforts have made this book possible—the Schimper Foundation, *Architectural Record* and *The Modern Hospital,* members of the advisory committee of the competition, the jury, the participants in the competition, and the writers of the text.

The Editors

THE NATIONAL COMMITTEE ON THE AGING
G. Warfield Hobbs, *Chairman*

National Social Welfare Assembly, Inc.
Hugh R. Jackson, *President*
Robert E. Bondy, *Director*

Contents

SECTION I: THE HOME FOR THE AGED

1: Congregate Living for Older People

By Ollie A. Randall
Vice Chairman, National Committee on the Aging

Congregate living in a home for the aged means that a group of nonrelated elderly people live together in the same place, according to arrangements planned and administered by designated responsible persons. The buildings in which such people are housed are, as a rule, designed primarily to give shelter to older people who can no longer live independently in the community or remain in the homes of their families or friends. Such homes, whether under public or voluntary auspices, were for many years the only resource provided by the community for the needy aged. Homes for the aged have always been regarded as an essential in any community's facilities for "sheltered care" of older citizens.

It is not strange that this social institution is becoming sensitive to the impact of dynamic forces that are constantly and rapidly changing the shape, not only of the future, but of the present. The home for the aged, in common with some other institutions, has frequently been characterized by its static quality—an immutable attitude and mode of operation, and an apparent unresponsiveness to the changes taking place around it. It has also been slow to understand that the management of its services can no longer remain independent of population trends, the reorganization of business and industry as well as of whole communities, and the new role of government—federal, state, and local—in supplying funds and services for the older members of our society.

It is impossible to evade the implications of these trends without sacrificing the quality of service that is so urgently needed by the individual and the community today. Unfortunately, new concepts, facilities, and services geared to present and future needs have been slow in developing. There is no room for complacency on the part of anyone concerned with the well-being of older people.

Public homes

It is important to remember that homes for the aged under public auspices were originally (and in many places still are) the town, county, or state poor farms. The major reasons elderly people sought shelter in the poor farm were lack of money or of family (who could supply either money or a place to live), or else some physical or mental handicap that deprived them of a rightful place in the family household or the community at large. But here were sent not only the poor, but misfits of all kinds, and even vagrants with no legitimate claim on the local government. Residents were (and in many places, even now, are) "committed," and regarded as the social and economic dregs of the community. The standards of care and service were generally low and rudimentary. Little thought was given to more than feeding and clothing the residents, and giving them a share in the work of the home and the farm on which it was situated, if they were physically fit to do anything at all.

Fortunately, there is now a better understanding of the causes of illness, physical and mental, and of dependency, and this understanding is reflected in better standards of care. Public homes today are often so organized as to administer services and care that equal or exceed in professional quality those of some homes under voluntary auspices. Nevertheless, the negative emotional connotations of being a public charge in a public institution persist to such an extent that the stigma attached is almost as strong as it ever was, and remains difficult to overcome.

The home under voluntary auspices

The voluntary home for the aged is distinguished from the public home by the fact that the support required in addition to the fees paid by residents is derived from voluntary contributions, dues of membership groups, or from endowments established by a philanthropist or a charitable organization rather than from taxes. These homes are usually provided for the benefit of members of a given congregation or parish, society, or community. They too were originally established primarily for the purpose of giving shelter and food to those accepted for residence from the time of admission until death.

The chief difference between the voluntary and the public home lies not in fundamental purpose but rather in the fact that the financial resources of the voluntary home permit a high degree of selectivity in the admission of residents that is impossible in a tax-supported program of any kind. This can be the source of great satisfaction to those who are accepted, and of irritation and disappointment to those who seek and are denied admission through failure to meet very restrictive eligibility requirements pertaining to age, sex, race, religious affiliation, place of residence, social status (interpreted by the admission committee on its own terms), vocation, nationality, and so on. Financial selectivity is exercised when a specific amount and method of payment is required.

The most difficult admission requirement to meet has often been that of "good" health. In the past, few of the homes, either voluntary or public, were well-enough equipped to admit persons in need of medical or nursing care, and many applicants had health problems serious enough to disqualify them.

A "home" as a home

A home means many things to many people, but perhaps the one requirement on which most would agree is that the place in which a person lives be one in which he feels "at home," in which he knows he belongs, and in which he has meaning to himself and to others who live under the same roof with him.

Feelings of satisfaction and belonging are created, primarily, not by the building, but rather by the quality of the life lived in the building and the relationships established within it. Yet it is becoming obvious that when life in the home is carried on in a building designed to permit the individual resident to follow a daily pattern of living that meets his personal needs (within the limits inevitably imposed by group living), there is greater peace of mind for that individual and greater harmony for the group of which he is a part.

The most encouraging trend in congregate living is the recognition that the older person *is* a person, and has desires and yearnings that deserve attention and respect; that life in the home should allow as much gratification of these feelings as possible; and that the home should make the effort to fit its accommodations and services to the individual, rather than insisting, as has been done so frequently and uncompromisingly in the past, that the individual be obliged to make a one-sided adjustment to the rules and regulations of the home.

This growing change in attitude owes much, obviously, to a growing acceptance of the fact that older people do not, just because they are older, lose the need for the very essence and spirit of life in a family home. Rather this need is increased as other means of satisfying the personal and emotional demands of daily living are reduced or disappear altogether. And so, in planning buildings that are to house older people in congregate settings, much thought is being given to what actually constitutes the minor and major activities that fill the hours of the individuals and of the group as a whole—both the residents and the staff. Although life in a home for the aged is, at best, a substitute for the kind of life one hopes to have in the intimacy of a family circle, thoughtful planning can make it a very rewarding substitute.

While it is clear that a building alone, no matter how well planned, cannot endow a home with the quality of life that its occupants want, it nevertheless has the potential for promoting that quality by its enabling provisions. The provision that represents perhaps the most radical departure from the procedures of earlier days is that of privacy for the older person, so long as he is at all able to conduct himself in the residence without any major difficulty for himself or for others. Many designs have indicated the genuine appreciation of planners of this very fundamental need, and of the flexibility required to allow for the individuality that is more, rather than less, sharply pronounced as people grow older.

Population increases in the older age group and changes in the age and state of health of those seeking admission to homes have a profound effect on living arrangements for older people. Although the proportion of older people living in institutions has not noticeably increased during the past few years, their total number has greatly increased, and more and more individuals must be served. While the new financial resources available may provide for the individual's basic needs of food, clothing, and shelter, and thus allow him to live alone, other needs dictate the preference for congregate living for a large number of older persons.

The group seeking admission to either voluntary or public homes is now largely much older and much less able-bodied than that accepted for admission in the past. Thus many homes have been obliged to adapt their admission practices to meet the new demands. They have accepted more of the infirm, feeble, and chronically invalided or ill than in the past. This fact has special significance for the planning and administration of the home—a greater proportion of accommodations must be infirmary beds; a greater part of the staff must be skilled in the care of patients; and a higher cost of operation will ensue. But it has also a very new meaning for the older person and for his family, if he has one.

The older person who is aware of impaired health and who is apprehensive about the future because of lack of sufficient funds for medical and nursing care, or because of the lack of appropriate facilities for care in the event of need, is now turning to the home for personal and health security. He is either alone or is with a family who cannot—and perhaps should not—undertake either the personal or the financial burden of care. One great challenge for the home is to provide the proper accommodations and services for this group. An even more vital challenge is to organize accommodations, services, and the daily program of living so that medical and nursing care do not dominate the home to such an extent that the "home" atmosphere disappears.

Achieving the proper balance between the demands for care of the feeble, the sick, and the mildly confused elderly residents on the one hand, and the genuine need for a healthy, normal environment that gives the individual the sense of being "at home" on the other, is a difficult task, but it is the criterion by which the home must be judged. The thought that goes into the planning, not only of the rooms that assure the individual resident maximum independence, but also of those rooms in which he must live if invalidism, illness, or handicap so require, will contribute much to the spiritual as well as to the physical well-being of the individual and the entire resident group.

Facilities must be provided for all residents,

regardless of health status, for many of the activities that in a normal living situation may be found outside the home. Privacy for individuals who have visitors, and flexibility in arrangements for having visitors, such as are characteristic of a person's own home, are of vital importance. The opportunity for social contacts, for religious worship, for satisfying individual interests, must exist within the home for those who cannot move out into the community. It must also be kept in mind that if the life in the home is to have the flavor of normality there must also be opportunities for engaging in the activities of the community for those who can and wish to do so, and for bringing the community into the home without formality. These procedures may disrupt the smooth operation of an "institution," but the administrator with a desire to imbue daily living with the necessary qualities will make every use of the accommodations the building offers to reach this goal of a home-like atmosphere.

General attitudes

There is an apparent deepening appreciation on the part of the general public of what "aging" means in terms of personal and public responsi-

bility for the lives of older people who, through no fault of their own, cannot adequately cope with their own problems. This appreciation gives rise to real hope and encouragement for the future improvement of facilities for congregate living. Older people and their families are beginning to realize how short the supply is of such facilities—at least facilities that offer services and programs they would want for themselves and members of their families.

Because of this realization, and the dissatisfaction with present arrangements, there is developing a new and informed body of citizens who support the use of public and private funds for the improvement of buildings or facilities, and for underwriting the costs of better qualitative standards for the services that are made available. This new sensitivity to the nature of the needs of older people, and of the genuinely humane quality required in congregate living, is an asset in the drive to meet modern needs in a modern way. Perhaps the day is not too far distant when this "home away from home" will in every sense be for older people what Carl Sandburg so aptly calls the true "center of things."

2: Community Needs and Resources

By Geneva Mathiasen
Executive Secretary, National Committee on the Aging

It is no longer possible for any group planning services for older people to proceed without relating to what other groups in the community are doing or may be persuaded to do.

Until very recently the only organized facility for meeting the needs of elderly people was a home for the aged. The more acceptable home was usually provided by religious or fraternal groups to take care of "their own." The county home provided for the indigent not eligible for any other home.

This haphazard approach worked well enough in an earlier day, but recent developments have necessitated a drastic change in the methods of meeting the needs of older people, based on total community planning.

Several factors have brought about this change. One is the sheer force of numbers. In 1900, when life expectancy was about 48, comparatively few people lived long enough to need special care. In a time when most of the country could be classified as rural or village, houses were bigger and families more closely knit, and those older people who needed a home could be taken in by some member of the family and could often pay for their "keep" by helping with chores.

Before the miracles of modern medicine conquered infectious diseases, long, lingering illnesses requiring hospital care were relatively infrequent. Now, with life expectancy at birth increased to over 70, with a population mostly housed in small homes and apartments and household chores much reduced, with families widely scattered, and with small town neighborliness superseded by professional "services" in urban and suburban areas, the situation of elderly people has changed greatly.

Consequently, many large cities and some small ones have established some central planning body to investigate the needs of older people in the community and to provide some means of help. The responsibility for such a group usually rests with councils of social agencies, if they exist. Otherwise, county welfare departments, mayors' committees, or independent citizens' groups may assume the leadership. A number of states also maintain committees or commissions, some of which help communities to solve their local problems in various ways. The federal government too, through its Federal Council on Aging and the special staff on aging in the Department of Health, Education and Welfare, recognizes the need for coordination and planning at the highest government level.

A number of religious and other philanthropic groups have established national advisory headquarters for work with the aged. The National Committee on the Aging brings all these interests together for study and planning, and provides a central information and consultation service with a special library of information and recorded observations on programs for older people as carried out in all parts of the country.

No individual or group can safely plan a home for the aged, or any other kind of service for older people, without reference to some of these community planning bodies through which information can be secured about both needs and resources.

First is the question of state requirements. Every state has some kind of legal standard for nursing and convalescent homes, and in most states nonprofit homes for the aged are included among the institutions governed by the licensing law or some other categories of state regulation such as those pertaining to visitation and supervision. Before any practical steps in planning and design can be undertaken, such state regulations must be known. The licensing authority, usually the state department of health or welfare, will welcome consultation, preferably before any specific plans are developed. Not one of the basic questions about planning a home can be answered without thinking in community-wide terms.

Any group planning a home should first find out whether the community maintains a planning group for services for the aged, and then determine how the home would be integrated with those services. It is probable that some sort of community survey may be needed. If so, the appropriate group may have to be persuaded to undertake it. If such a survey has already been made, the information will be invaluable to a group interested in providing congregate care. If no central planning body exists, consultations with community welfare directors, departments of health, doctors and hospital administrators, visiting nurses, ministers, and the like will provide some information about local needs and help give answers to some basic questions.

Admission policy

Is the home to serve only members of a particular group, or is it to be open to all on the basis of need? Are only the well and ambulatory to be admitted, or will those with chronic illness or disability also be welcome? If only the well are admitted, what will happen to residents when they become ill? What about those who are senile or may become so? Once the admission policy is decided upon, who is to determine each applicant's eligibility?

These questions can of course be answered only after a knowledge of other community resources has been acquired. Today most authorities believe that a home for the aged is for those who for one reason or another need some degree of sheltered care; that an infirmary should be an integral part of the home, available to residents if and when they need it; that residents should be sent to the hospital only for acute illness; and that both resident and hospital should be assured that the patient will return to the home as soon as the need for hospital care has ended.

Admission policies in any situation, however, will inevitably be affected by the availability of other health facilities. If a community has either a chronic disease hospital or a chronic disease wing of a general hospital with empty beds, available to elderly patients at a price they are able to pay, plans for the infirmary of the home may be simplified. If the planning group is inclined toward a policy of caring only for minor illnesses and mishaps, such a decision cannot be made without prior investigation of the availability, standards, and costs of alternate facilities in the community such as nursing and convalescent homes. It is wise for policy-making groups of the home and other health agencies to consult together, before building, about their respective admission policies, in order to work out an agreement for emergency or acute care. Many hospitals are reluctant to accept elderly patients unless assured of a satisfactory arrangement for their discharge, at the suitable time, without undue delay.

A change is also taking place in the admission procedure. It is no longer wise to leave decisions entirely to untrained people. Hence, there is a growing use of trained social workers to investigate the background and current situation of the applicant in relation to the admission policies of the home, the kind of care it is equipped to give, and so on. The social worker's task is to help the applicant and members of his family reach the proper decision on entering the home, and also to help ease problems of adjustment to congregate living if they occur.

Nearly all large, progressive homes now employ social workers as staff members. If such a staff position is not feasible or desirable, arrangements may be made with a family agency in the community to assume the function of screening applicants and making recommendations on admission (both to the applicant and to the home) in the light of total community resources and the individual's need. Some communities have a central bureau or referral agency for the aged that may aid in admission procedures. Or, in larger communities, several homes may jointly employ a trained social worker in order to develop admission procedures on a professional basis.

Size

The size of the home can be correctly determined only in relation to both current and future needs. Maximum goals should be considered at the outset, and plans for possible expansion should be included in the original design, no matter how small the building is to be at first. Such foresight may avoid costly mistakes when expansion does become necessary. To determine the appropriate size, one must know first of all: (1) The potential number of residents needing such a facility, (2) Their own preferences about how and where they live, (3) How much choice the community will offer, and (4) How much money can be secured for building.

Location

There are obviously many factors, involving total community plans, to be considered in making the crucial decision of where to locate the home. These are considered in detail in Chap. 3. For example, a city plan with zoning regulations may make it very difficult to reconcile the needs of the older residents for a suitable place to live with over-all ideas for city development and expansion. Surely, consultation with planning authorities should be one of the first steps in considering a home for the aged. It is important to know not only the current situation but what appear to be trends or possibilities for future expansion—location of industries, residential communities, and the like.

Important, too, is a decision on what limitations, if any, will be imposed on applicants' eligibility because of geographic origin. Policies vary widely in this respect. Some groups plan national homes, designed to care for members who may come from any part of the country. This method is used particularly for homes planned by union, fraternal, and some nationality groups. Most religious denominations maintain homes in various parts of the country, but an analysis of their locations indicates little central planning on the basis of need or geographical distribution. Some religious groups do plan for homes on a regional basis, particularly when the constituency of one community does not have enough potential residents to warrant a plant of economical size, either for building or administration, so that joint planning is required by all communities engaged in the venture.

Other groups prefer to maintain homes within each community, even though they may be small and lack some of the amenities and services of the larger institution. This preference is based on the belief that it is important for older people to remain among familiar surroundings close to relatives and friends. If this procedure is followed it is obviously necessary to rely more heavily on other community resources to care for health, recreation, and other needs that might be an integral part of a large plant.

Services

It has been adequately demonstrated that it is no longer necessary for an elderly person to retire from active living upon entering a home for the aged. The old concept of a rocking-chair existence as typical of an old people's home is (in theory, at least) a thing of the past. For good mental and physical health, participation—to the very end if possible—is the keynote. This consideration adds a new dimension to planning a modern home.

If the residents are to participate in a lively program of activities, receive guests and make visits, give small parties, play games, take walks, garden, work at handicrafts, serve the Red Cross or other community effort, participate in public worship, read and study, join discussion groups —then obviously these activities must be provided for in the planning. Is the home to be a self-contained unit providing for all these activities within its own walls and grounds, or are there community facilities that can be used?

Take the matter of public worship, for example. The size of the chapel may be determined by the nearness of other churches, and ease of transportation to them. The cooperation of the churches may be sought in advance, particularly if the group to be served is interdenominational. Is there a community plan for transporting elderly and infirm members to and from church? Are there special programs and activities in which they may take part? Can chaplains be supplied for those who are homebound? Or does worship outside the home present such problems as to indicate the advisability of planning for major religious services to be held in the home itself? And if so, who will conduct the services? The cooperation of a single church or pastor or of a ministerial association may have to be secured.

The nearness to and relationship with a public library may determine the responsibility of the home in providing books. If there is a public library within walking distance of ambulatory residents, the demands on the size and character of the library in the home will be greatly reduced. If, in addition, the public library has a bookmobile, a traveling library service, or will provide books for a weekly book cart for the nonambulatory, and a volunteer to man the service, the responsibility of the home will be minimal.

If there is an activity center for older people near the home that will welcome its residents, it may be desirable to encourage them to join it, but residents must not be deprived of suitable activities in the home. If, on the other hand, there is no place in the community where older people can take part in social and educational activities, the home may well consider making its own facilities available to community groups. Or, there may be a sharing of facilities. For example, the home may provide an auditorium for dramatics and concerts, while some other agency may provide both the equipment and teachers for pottery or other handicraft.

This kind of foresight is, of course, crucial in planning medical and rehabilitation services. A few homes find it preferable to provide a complete medical service, and actually achieve the status of medical institutions. Short of such a step, the kind and extent of medical care to be given within the home must be related to other facilities that care for acute and chronic illness within the community.

There have been many demonstrations of how a close working relationship between a general hospital and a home for the aged can result in better and more economical patient care. Arrangements may be made for the hospital to provide a visiting staff of doctors to serve the home; or to admit residents for emergency care on a priority basis; or to make available its outpatient services to residents of the home, to provide special services such as X-ray, laboratory, pharmacy, and the like; or to provide regular physical check-ups or diagnostic examinations; or to participate in joint research programs; and so on.

While these arrangements are perhaps more easily achieved when both home and hospital are under the same general auspices, the closest possible integration of the medical services of the home with all other health facilities in the community should be sought by the policy-making boards of the several agencies in the early stages of planning. The degree of cooperation and integration will determine the nature of medical facilities provided by the home and therefore the architectural plan.

Costs and financing

How much will the home cost and how will it be financed? Community relationships can affect: (1) The financing of the building itself, and (2) The meeting of operating costs.

Federal and state legislation in recent years have made possible matching grants and long-term, low-interest loans to nonprofit groups for erecting housing for the aged, chronic disease hospitals, nursing homes, and rehabilitation units. Nonprofit groups may find it desirable to consult the U.S. Public Health Service and the Housing and Home Finance Agency of the federal government regarding the availability of loans or matching grants, and the standards required of buildings constructed with the aid of federal financing. A few states have also taken similar steps in supplying financial aid to nonprofit groups that provide housing and sheltered care for older people.

The traditional policy of payment by a resident of a lump sum at admission for which the home contracted to provide life care is rapidly being replaced by monthly payments on a cost-of-care basis. Therefore, the available amount of Old Age and Survivors Insurance benefits and Old Age Assistance grants becomes increasingly important in relation to the operating budget of the home.

The incomes of older people are likely to be derived from these sources plus private pensions, annuities, and other forms of personal savings. If a home is to provide service on the basis of need rather than ability to pay the total cost of care, the income level of the residents will determine the amount of endowment or income other than residents' payments necessary to meet costs.

Old Age Assistance is provided to elderly people without income on a means-test basis. The amount of the grant varies from state to state and even from one locality to another within the state. The funds are a combination of federal and state contributions, often supplemented by the local community. The rate of payment to recipients of Old Age Assistance residing in a home is often determined by the kind and quality of care, as well as the type of accommodation, furnished the individual. If, as often occurs, the amount of Old Age and Survivors Insurance benefits for older people is below the Old Age Assistance level, the difference may be made up by funds from Old Age Assistance.

This fact is of great importance to homes for the aged. As people continue to live longer, the life care payments that have been made in earlier years are often insufficient to provide for the unexpected added years. Private savings, of course, are subject to the same inadequacy. When personal resources are exhausted, many homes help their residents secure the Old Age Assistance benefits that enable them to pay part or all of the cost of care. This procedure demands a close relationship between the local department of welfare and the management of the home. In the earliest stages of planning, the amount of income to be derived from recipients of Old Age Assistance may influence the extent of the facilities to be provided.

3: Location and Building Site

By John Park Lee
Director, Division of Welfare Agencies, Board of Pensions of the Presbyterian Church in the U.S.A.

Every resident in a home for the aged should be encouraged and assisted to strive for active participation in community life and for personal growth and development. The residents' success in attaining these ends depends largely on the location and building site of the home or colony in which they live.

Those planning a home for older people will find that there is no all-purpose location or site, no place that is perfect in every respect. Compromises must be made. A most desirable spot may be too costly. A healthful location may not have good transportation service. A beautiful site may be too far from shopping and recreational facilities. The planning group must try to find a place that combines as many as possible of the desirable features without completely sacrificing any one of them.

Living in a rural setting at a considerable distance from city facilities is not usually recommended, although it might be desirable in special circumstances. Planning groups often acquire such a property because they are attracted by its low price or because it is offered as a gift. As a result, they unintentionally subject the residents in the home built on the property to what may be a very dull life, with no activity going on around the home, few visitors because of its remoteness, and little chance to get out because of difficulties in traveling to a town. It is true that such locations are healthful and quiet, but these advantages may actually be negated by the dullness and lack of stimulation that accompany them. Planning committees are usually composed of active, vigorous, hardworking men and women for whom the quiet of a rustic scene has great charm, but they tend to forget that country living is particularly difficult and lonely for those unused to it. Complete quiet is both undesirable for and undesired by most aged people.

Living in the heart of a big city has its attractions. Everything needed is close at hand; life goes forward all around the home with an exciting rush and movement that is stimulating just to watch; family, friends, and others can visit easily. On the other hand, it is hard for older people to take an afternoon nap if the street outside is noisy; some are afraid to venture out because of the heavy traffic flowing by; there is a good deal of heat in the summer and dirt when the windows are open; and city property is costly.

A compromise between far-out country and way-in city—location in a suburban area or in a small city—is a good solution. Both offer facilities to cater to almost every need. Both usually have good transportation; activities that promote personal growth; grass, trees, flowers, birds, and attractive natural settings; and properties available at reasonable prices.

Location

Accessibility   Accessibility is the first important consideration in determining the location of a home.

The home must be easily accessible from the central section of its community, preferably by public transportation for residents, staff, and visitors—members of the board, the families of residents, representatives of the group supporting the home (church, lodge, union, and the like), professional men such as physicians, and other service people. The more easily the home is reached, the greater will be the flow of activity through it, and consequently the greater the stimulus to those living there.

Not all of those who wish to visit a home, or who must reach it in the course of their work, have automobiles. Good public transportation —rail, bus, or trolley—at modest prices and at frequent intervals is therefore a necessity. If such facilities do not exist the home will have to furnish transportation by station wagon or bus at its own expense.

It is also desirable that the community in which the home is situated be itself accessible. Some homes are now in communities that were once situated on public transportation routes but that now are not even served by bus lines. For people without cars, visiting such homes is a serious problem. No planning committee can be sure that train, bus, or trolley lines will not be discontinued, but a fairly accurate guess can be made about the chances for various communities to be cut off from such transportation in the future.

Proximity   A home for the aged should be near the following: stores, theaters, libraries, churches and synagogues, hospitals, physicians, dentists and other health resources, sport and recreational facilities, and a center of population from which staff can be drawn.

Nearness to stores is important. Everyone needs toilet articles and similar items from the drug store. Stationery and stamps, reading matter, clothing and knickknacks, and presents for friends must be bought. Window shopping is fun even if nothing is bought.

The movies, theatre, and concerts are a great delight to many older people, and the absence of these activities may work a real hardship.

Radio and television have become almost essential for all ages today, but especially for residents in homes for older people. Virtually no area today is without at least one radio station, but some communities still lack television. Good television reception, with as many channels as possible, is desirable when choosing a location.

Reading is an almost universal pleasure of older people, and the home should, of course, make books available to residents. However, it is impossible for a home to stock, or for residents to buy, all the materials that might be found in a library, such as professional journals, reference works, and the like. The necessity to visit an outside library may have its rewards, for such activity is often stimulating and enjoyable for older people; but the visit must be made an easy one for them to make, and their new home should be built as near a library as possible.

Many homes provide worship services within their walls, and these services can be helpful and comforting for those who cannot leave the home. But it is far better for the residents to worship at a community church or synagogue and become working members of a congregation. The good and rounded religious life consists in far more than listening to sermons, following liturgies, and reading sacred passages. At its best, it means active participation in the life of the congregation—joining with it in all its activities as well as in its periods of worship.

The residents of a home near churches and synagogues can belong to men's and women's associations, join in discussion and reading groups, sew or make bandages for the Red Cross, assist the Community Chest in mailing out campaign letters, serve on official boards and committees, and so on.

Congregations can use a great many of the skills that older people have—a retired businessman can keep a church's books, for example, and others can help with mailings and keeping

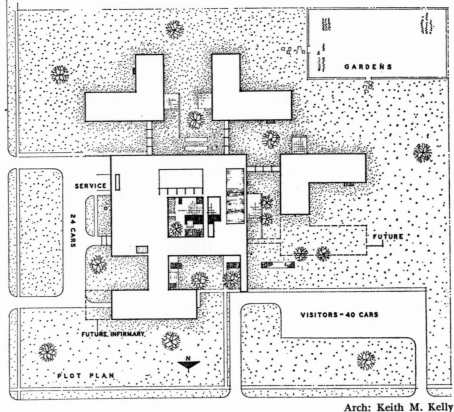

Arch: Keith M. Kelly

The development of this site has been dominated by the right angle, and one wishes that the designer had achieved a pattern less reminiscent of the surrounding gridiron street plans, so as to provide a greater contrast for the building. The site is not large but appears adequate for this single-story building. Like many other such plans, planted areas have been introduced between and within the individual buildings to provide vistas and a feeling of openness and space that would be utterly destroyed were this a single, continuous building envelope with all its component parts inside.

The two parking lots are so dissimilar and so awkward as to make one question the designer's knowledge of automobiles. However, they are well related to the building and to each other. Service and ambulance entrances relate well to the other parts of the home.

various kinds of attendance records. Members of the congregation and residents can profit by the closer relationships that can best be fostered if they are near each other.

Residents of a home for the aged must be able to visit their doctors' and dentists' offices. These professional offices should be close by for the benefit of not only the residents but also of those professional men who will gladly call at homes for older people if they are relatively near. Unfortunately, hospitalization of older people because of accidents, cerebral and cardiac failure, and other reasons, is fairly frequent. It is much easier for the home to develop a good working relationship with a general hospital if it is near at hand.

It is most desirable for the hospital to be a teaching hospital whose professors and medical students will welcome the opportunity to treat and study older patients. Many older people gladly participate in research projects when their purpose is explained. Such participation makes them feel important.

Play should be a vital part of life in later years. The home should be near at least some of the following public sport and recreational facilities for both spectators and participants: baseball parks, shuffleboard courts, football stadia, bowling greens, boxing and wrestling arenas, chess and checker clubs, basketball gymnasia, bridge and samba parties, swimming pools, croquet fields, orchestra and band concerts, and instrumental and choral groups.

Here again, while each home should have its own recreational facilities, it is far better for the residents' development to participate with others in the community. It is even better for the home when its own glee club or drama group or the like goes out into the community to entertain others.

The home should be near a center of population large enough to provide a source from which most of the staff can be drawn. Executive staff may be brought in from elsewhere. For the development of a sense of community, it helps to have the bulk of those employed in the home living in the community of which the home is a part. Before making a final decision the planning group should consult with employment agencies and state or federal employment services to determine whether staff can be recruited nearby.

Finally, a home should be planned with due regard to the interests of its supporters. If, for example, the home is related to a church, it should be situated in an area where members of that church are living. If it is to be directed by a labor union, it should be near the homes and working places of those in the union still actively employed. If it is to be made up of members of some professional group—ministers or teachers, for example—it would be wise to locate it near some center of the same type of professional activity, such as a seminary or a college or university.

Integration   The home may be accessible to the outside world; it may be near many desirable services and attractions; but it must be a part of the community itself, a community in which all sorts of people of all ages, engaged in all kinds of work, are living.

While it is true that there are times when older people wish to be with their contemporaries, it is not true that they wish to be confined to live exclusively with them. Too often older people have been segregated because of age in ways that have had just as unfortunate effects on them as segregation for other reasons has had on other minority groups.

Integration benefits other segments of the community, too. For example, young people and children need to be with and see older people. In modern housing developments there are too often only young adults and their children. There is no room in most modern houses for grandparents. It is essential that, wherever possible, homes for the aging be established in an area where families of all kinds and ages are living.

Most older people enjoy children and some may be able to supplement their limited incomes by baby sitting if the families they are to serve are not too far away. Children provide an enormous stimulus to older people, and help to keep them flexible and in touch with modern life.

Separation   The home must be built away from disturbing and distracting influences that do not stimulate but merely annoy, distress, or imperil.

No home should be situated near a large factory that emits noise, smoke, and fumes. Nor should the planners build where there is likely to be a great deal of dust. If dust is unavoidable, a screen of trees is almost a necessity. The home should not be built on heavy traffic arteries, and

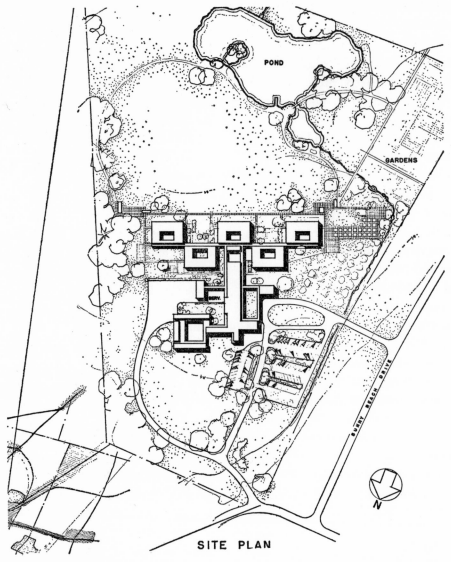

SITE PLAN

Arch: Adam & Lee

The lot appears large enough, is flat, and has the charm of a small pond towards the south. Access from a quiet residential street is direct, but the parking development, although adequate in size and well located for expansion, is somewhat circuitous of access. An excellent idea is the planting area between the parking lanes.

The service entrance is well located, and the service drive serves also as an ambulance access road. Most of the residence units face towards the south and the pond, but some turn back towards the more active areas of the building, providing a range of room views from remote to intimate. The area around the buildings has been paved, and the pavement serves generally as a transition from building to lawn as well as for wheelchair use. The south lawn, the pond, the gardening area, and the buildings are linked by a meandering path that is a very pleasant feature.

if it is a multibuilding home it should be designed so that the residents do not have to cross heavily traveled streets to reach the main building from the other buildings or cottages.

Climate   It must not be assumed that all older people want to live in a warm, semitropical climate. Many like cold winters, and would miss snow and ice. The climate to which prospective residents are accustomed should be considered in selecting the location of their future home.

Areas with sudden and violent temperature shifts or excessive humidity should be avoided. Prevailing winds must also be considered. If they blow steadily at a fairly high rate, they will make living difficult for older people. Walking against a strong wind is tiring and may induce a heart attack. Walking with strong gusts of wind against the back may cause a fall.

It is desirable to have enough rainfall to make grass, plants, and flowers grow, to keep the water table high, and reservoirs full. But excessive dampness causes difficulty for some arthritic and bronchial cases, as well as mildew in shoes and other clothing.

Regions characterized by severe freezing and icing, which make walking hazardous for long periods of time, should be avoided.

Building site

Size   The type of home and its location will determine the size of the building site to be acquired.

Obviously, a home in a large city where property values are high will use as little land as is necessary to conform to local building codes or zoning restrictions. Such a home will obtain space by building vertically rather than horizontally. On the other hand, homes in suburban areas or small cities where land costs are more reasonable can acquire and hold more property.

If the home is to be a colony—a collection of small cottages or buildings—or a combination of colony and congregate home with both cottages and central building, more land will be needed than for a straight congregate-type home. It is wise to avoid the acquisition of large acreage that will require an extensive and expensive maintenance staff. Spacious lawns are charming, but are expensive to develop, mow, and maintain. Four to five acres should prove adequate for the average congregate-type home, and would permit the addition of a few cottages or apartments if this type of facility is desired.

Of course, the planning committee should keep future needs in mind. If the home is planned eventually to be a large one, but is to start modestly by housing only 25 residents, the committee members should make certain that there will be enough space to permit later expansion until the maximum number of residents is reached. If enough funds are on hand at the outset to permit the erection of a home that will not have to be expanded later on, the land needs can be planned accordingly.

The grounds should be spacious enough to permit the residents some activity—croquet, bowling, gardening, cook-outs, and the like—but not so large that they become a burden to maintain.

If the plot is adequate, the home will be protected against encroachment, but it may be impossible to achieve this end if the home is to be built in a large city where land values require the use of virtually all the available space.

Topography   The topography of a prospective building site must be carefully considered. For example, it is helpful to obtain expert advice on subsoil conditions. Can cellars be dug without encountering ground water? Will the land drain? Can septic tanks be used effectively? Is there a ledge of rock beneath the topsoil that will make the cost of a cellar prohibitive? Determining the answers to these and similar questions in advance may avoid much expense and trouble later on.

The ground should be level, or have at most a very gentle slope. The site should not be on the top of a hill, in a narrow valley, or on the side of a hill where residents would have to walk

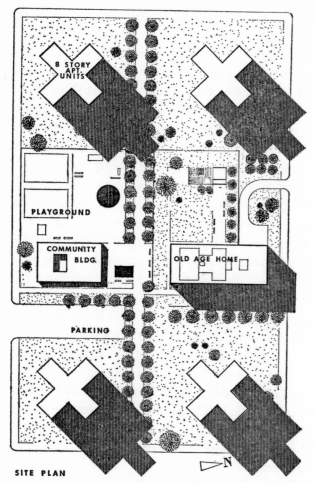

SITE PLAN

Arch: Smith, Yauch, & Schreiber

This urban project reflects contemporary thinking for high-density developments. It would be easy to imagine that all aspects of city dwelling were here—the roar of traffic, the bus lines, and the like. And yet it is equally easy to imagine that this one block might provide a pleasantly relaxing environment. There would "never be a dull moment" in this home—a desirable feature for those who have lived this way all their lives and for whom quiet and isolation accelerate the aging process. Here one must eventually die of nervous exhaustion rather than of boredom. Interest and excitement will be provided by neighborhood mothers and children, ball games and dances, and use of the home and its facilities.

This arrangement of buildings symbolizes the rejection of withdrawal as a pattern for the aging. Life teems all around the home, and one has only to step outside to take part in it.

up or down to get to and from the home. It must be remembered that a high altitude may pose a medical problem for some older people (because the rarefied atmosphere places an added burden on lungs and heart).

Grass, trees, flowers, and other growing things are a necessity. The soil should be reasonably fertile so that the residents may, if they desire, cultivate their own flower or vegetable gardens, and so that the home can maintain lawns, trees, and shrubbery without great expense for fertilizer, topsoil, and the like.

Every advantage should be taken of the natural characteristics of the site. Preservation of large or unusual trees may make new construction take on a settled appearance. Key rooms in the home may be oriented toward a view, and if it is worth the effort, the whole building plan may be shaped so that the greatest number of residents share it. These views need not be scenic; older people enjoy watching activities, such as children at play in a school yard, or traffic on a busy street.

It must always be remembered that it is foolish to destroy the natural attractions of a site, especially when these may have been the deciding factor when purchasing the land.

Zoning restrictions   Committees often find desirable sites in areas restricted by law to single-family units, or with severe space limitations on multiple dwelling units. Zoning authorities should be consulted before any property is purchased, or even optioned, to make certain that if zoning laws are restrictive exceptions will be granted, and that the community will permit the erection of a home for older people. This

1. "CENTER" FOR AGING
2. RESIDENTIAL UNITS
3. HOUSES
4. APARTMENTS
5. STORES
6. COMMUNITY PLAYHOUSE
7. BIBLE SEMINARY
8. HIGH SCHOOL
9. ADULT EDUCATION CENTER
10. MUNICIPAL GOLF COURSES
11. CASTING POOL
12. RECREATIONAL & PICNIC AREAS
13. PROPOSED PUBLIC CROSSINGS
14. LAGOON
15. CHURCH
16. 3 MILES TO CENTER OF TOWN
17. ONE MILE TO COMMUNITY HOSP.
18. FUTURE COMMUNITY BUILDINGS

BUILDINGS FOR THE AGING
FUTURE EXPANSION
EXIST. RESIDENCES AND STORES
EXIST. COMMUNITY BUILDINGS

SITE PLAN
0 100 300 600
N

Arch: Lombardo

This plan demonstrates a careful analysis of such things as public transportation routes, utilities, and community services. Such a study should always be made before final selection of site.

The basic scheme portrayed is unusual in that it isolates the residential units from the home's central facilities. This method certainly places the residents in the community but it also loses the advantages of living in one building with everything under one roof. However, such decentralization can not infrequently yield a very attractive way of life.

step is usually taken while consulting with community planning bodies on other matters, as discussed under "Community planning," below.

Frontages   It is also important for the planning group to study the frontages of the prospective home and visualize the immediately adjacent aspects. If funds and available space permit, the ideal frontages (in a city or suburb) would be wide streets on all sides with no neighbor closer than across the street. Next in desirability would be streets on three or on two sides.

Utilities, fire protection, and other community services   Community services can materially affect the ease of operation of a home and the comfort of its residents.

The planning group must make sure that the proposed site is near an ample water supply, preferably city or suburban. Electricity is essential but will probably be available wherever the home is built. Cooking and heating require ample supplies of gas, oil, or coal, if electric power is not to be used for these functions. Is a gas main available, or will bottled gas have to be used? How costly are fuel oil and coal in the area? These questions must be considered in advance.

Fire and police protection for the home and its residents is essential. The type of fire company—volunteer or professional—and water lines available, will affect the safety of the residents and the cost of fire insurance. A community police force to guard against pilferage and vandalism and to protect the older people on their way to and from the home is also necessary. The planning committee should explore these matters with the local authorities.

Garbage and trash disposal are two more important concerns. If local government is not responsible for collecting this material, how is it

to be disposed of? Of course, there is no problem if the site selected enjoys this kind of service.

Sewage disposal is another vital problem that must be settled in advance. If the home can be linked to a city or suburban sewer system, well and good. If not, the planning group should obtain, through its architect, expert advice on the type of sewage disposal system to install. This decision will depend, in part, on the topography of the site.

Community planning   Community planning authorities should be consulted before a site is purchased. In many areas there are authorities or boards charged under the law with controlling development in and around cities. These groups are usually happy to discuss their plans and to advise on available sites in locations where homes and facilities are likely to appear. If a building committee has a site in mind, it should consult such groups to determine whether the erection of a home on that site will conform to the community development program.

If such development agencies do not exist, the planning group should consult with local authorities on its intentions and solicit their advice on acquisition of property.

Erection of a home for older people by a charitable, religious, or other nonprofit organization means the loss of property from the tax rolls. Some local communities do not view this prospect with equanimity. Opposition may develop from other residents of the community who mistakenly believe that erection of a home for older people will have a morbid effect on the life of the community and cause a corresponding lowering of property values. Planning groups must gauge the extent and intensity of these feelings. Sometimes such opposition yields to friendly and composed discussions.

4: Common Services

By Eli H. Rudin
Executive Director, Hebrew Home for the Aged, Boston, Massachusetts

The common rooms are the core of any type of congregate living. If a home for the aged is to be a "home" it must be one in which the residents are part of a communal society, although each remains at all times an individual personality. The privacy of his room permits the resident to maintain his individuality; the communal rooms allow residents to share ideas and experiences with others.

Living together, especially with strangers, requires adjustment and understanding. The common services must be planned and coordinated to contribute toward this end. The type of resident to be served, as established by the policy of the board of trustees, should always define what is to be provided in the way of congregate areas and services.

If the institution is to care primarily for the infirm, a special type of planning is necessary. The ambulant and healthy aged can utilize facilities more like those of a private home. The needs of the individuals to be served must always be the factor determining the extent to which the board, administrator, and architect plan for the communal areas.

It may not be necessary for each home to provide all of the services suggested in this chapter. If community services were available to residents of the home, for example, there might be no need for duplication. Perhaps a local community center, sheltered workshop, public library, or fraternal hall could be utilized to contribute toward a well-rounded program for congregate living.

Through careful development, the common areas can play a vital part in caring for the total needs of the resident as an individual. The individual may give as well as receive. Group communication can afford an incentive to become part of a living community as opposed to the deterioration to which continual privacy may lead. Normal living is one of balance and personal contact and should be the goal of our planning.

Common rooms

There must be an emphasis on small, intimate groupings. There can be privacy in the midst of activity. Provision should be made for the proper arrangement of furniture, lighting, and drapes within the common rooms so as to highlight the selectivity of friendship within the larger group. Attractive decor should be part of every room. It should blend the furnishings so as to minimize the institutional aspect. No longer are drab browns and tans vital to proper maintenance.

The architect should consider safety measures for each of the common areas as well as the bedrooms and bathrooms. For example, nurse calls, among other features, are important.

Living rooms

Living rooms fall into two categories—the main lounge in the central building, and the smaller living rooms located in or near the sleeping areas.

The main lounge should be near the main entrance but not part of a public lobby. The need for small groups and private conversations should be recognized. Residents should be able to talk with friends and relatives without having to move furniture from one part of the room to another.

The main lounge can be used by larger groups for recreational purposes such as films, concerts, plays, dances, and parties. A pantry should be located adjacent to the lounge, to facilitate the serving of refreshments and to encourage volunteer organizations to participate in the programs. The sharing of food can be of great help in breaking down barriers. Very little equipment is necessary other than that required for heating and storing food and washing and storing dishes.

Small living rooms should be located in or near the sleeping areas in sufficient number to provide for the residents of a specific wing or floor. These small rooms can be used for private or small group recreation—cards, music, radio, television, tea parties, letter writing, and smoking. (Because the presence of fire hazards requires constant vigilance, it is necessary to control smoking by residents and personnel. Such control is simpler when smoking is allowed only in special areas.)

A small adjacent pantry, with facilities for food heating and storage, encourages private entertainment and parties. Or individuals may just sit by themselves—a luxury in any group living situation, be it a nurses' dormitory, an army barracks, or a home for the aged.

The design of the home should ensure the accessibility and proximity of these rooms to the sleeping and dining areas. They can be of special value for use by the residents for dining under unusual circumstances, such as a temporary disability or infirmity. This procedure will reserve the infirmary rooms for more serious cases and add to the comfort of those who may

remain in their own surroundings—a decided aid to good morale and quicker recovery.

The lounges should always retain the informality and functional values of true living rooms, rather than be merely sitting rooms. Here can be shared the warmth of companionship during years of enjoyment, not just survival.

Dining rooms

Three meals a day—21 meals a week—1,095 meals a year—and more with snacks, teas, and parties! Through sheer force of usage, the dining rooms belong among the most important areas in the home.

The main dining room should be centrally located, near the kitchen, and with more than enough space to avoid crowding. It is desirable to have not more than four residents at one table, with provision for individual tables for couples. In addition, provision should be made for privacy for those residents unable to dine with others—residents who are embarrassed by infirmities, or who may have difficulty in eating properly.

The decoration and color scheme should make for more pleasurable dining. Soundproofing is necessary to reduce the noise of conversation, the clatter of dishes and cutlery, and the normal commotion of service. If possible, the diners should face a pleasant view.

The arrangement of tables should allow for wheelchairs and crutch walkers. Older persons need more room for movement; stumbles and falls must be anticipated. A small parking stand for crutches and canes will obviate the need for hanging them on the backs of chairs or placing them under tables, and thus prevent accidents.

Space for feeding occasional visitors should be provided. Also, future expansion of the dining area should be considered. If bedrooms are to be added at some later date, the dining area must be planned accordingly. Future additions might be blocked because of poor planning of the original dining and other service areas.

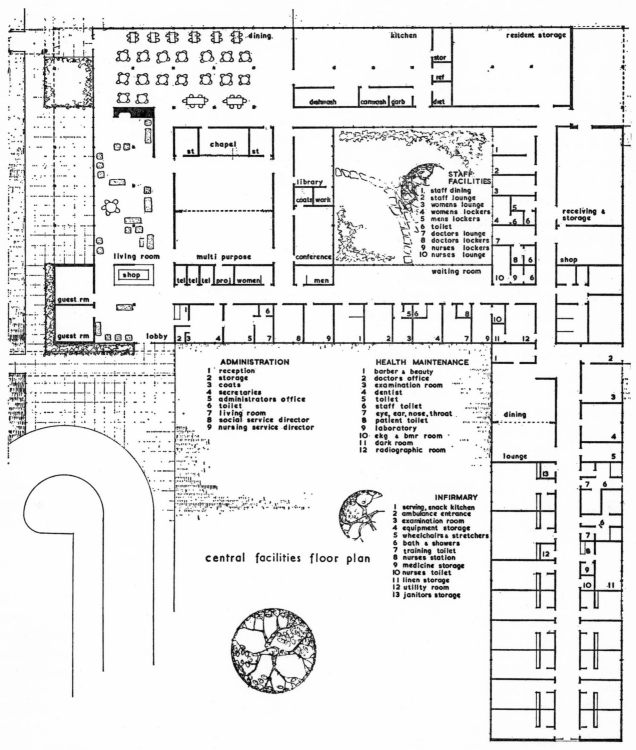

dining

kitchen

resident storage

stor

ref

dashwash | canwash | garb

diet

chapel

st | st

library

coats | work

conference

STAFF FACILITIES
1. staff dining
2. staff lounge
3. womens lounge
4. womens lockers
5. mens lockers
6. toilet
7. doctors lounge
8. doctors lockers
9. nurses lockers
10. nurses lounge

receiving & storage

shop

living room

multi purpose

shop

tel | tel | tel | proj | women

men

waiting room

guest rm

guest rm

lobby

dining

lounge

ADMINISTRATION
1. reception
2. storage
3. coats
4. secretaries
5. administrators office
6. toilet
7. living room
8. social service director
9. nursing service director

HEALTH MAINTENANCE
1. barber & beauty
2. doctors office
3. examination room
4. dentist
5. toilet
6. staff toilet
7. eye, ear, nose, throat
8. patient toilet
9. laboratory
10. ekg & bmr room
11. dark room
12. radiographic room

central facilities floor plan

INFIRMARY
1. serving, snack kitchen
2. ambulance entrance
3. examination room
4. equipment storage
5. wheelchairs & stretchers
6. bath & showers
7. training toilet
8. nurses station
9. medicine storage
10. nurses toilet
11. linen storage
12. utility room
13. janitors storage

Arch: R. L. Unruck

A very successful feature of this plan is the relationship between the entrance lobby and the main living room. Its open, informal character is helped by the way the reception desk (and hence the control and institutional aspect of the building) is played down.

Dining, multipurpose, chapel, and library rooms are logically sized and located. A nice feature is the placement of the conference room.

The recreation room

It may often be necessary to use the large living room for recreation, but if funds and space permit, a separate area for this purpose is preferable. This room should be adaptable to various kinds of programming—movies, dancing, lectures, concerts, festive meals, and the like. This multipurpose room should be capable of division into smaller areas.

Enough space should be provided for the storage of chairs, tables, and other equipment to be used for parties and special events. This consideration is all too easily overlooked. Storage space is important.

The recreation room should be usable by bed and wheelchair patients. Their participation in the normal routine is an important and vital factor in maintenance of patient morale. It is surprising how this practice is accepted by the more able-bodied residents, who always cooperate in making the infirm comfortable and a part of the total scene.

An amplifying system with earphones for the hard of hearing should be provided. The unit may be portable and can be used in other areas such as the dining room, patio, and infirmary. Savings can be effected if the wiring is installed at the time of construction, so that the unit may be simply connected at various points when amplification is required. The installation of television sets may present a special problem. While a central television area is desirable, the best system adds television outlets in every room, with central control.

Motion picture booths and equipment should be considered. Local building codes must be checked to determine whether fireproof booths are required. It is wise to use 35 mm. widescreen projectors so that the latest productions may be viewed. The 16 mm. films available are often too dated to justify their cost. However, provision for the showing of both types of film allows for flexibility of programming.

Religious services

Smaller homes may have to adapt the recreation room for use as a chapel, but separate arrangements for religious services are better. A small chapel may be built adjacent to the recreation room, with a sliding wall between. Emphasis should be on small meditation rooms rather than large, expensive chapels. These rooms must be part of the everyday living pattern and not just Sabbath day show pieces.

Religion is usually an intimately personal experience for the older individual, and the architect and trustees should plan accordingly.

The amplifying system and earphones for the deaf mentioned previously are important for religious services. If possible, this equipment should be connected to the over-all house paging system to relay the services to the room- or bed-ridden. Participation by listening has become a vital part of our everyday life.

The decorating scheme of the rooms set aside for worship and meditation should be appropriately restful. Permanent pews should be installed, if at all possible, but space should be provided for wheelchairs. Simplicity should be the keynote.

Garden and patio

The garden and patio should be a functional part of the total structure and must be considered in the over-all planning. The garden should be informal and "touchable," part of the home life itself. With proper shade, comfortable furniture, and space for outdoor sitting, the modern concept of bringing the out-of-doors into the house can be effected in the home for the aged as well as in ranch or split-level houses. Depending on the climate and location, concerts, picnics and cook-outs, shuffleboard, croquet, and other activities can take place in the garden.

Residents should be allowed to participate in garden maintenance. A green thumb does not pale with the years. With proper equipment, weeding can be done from a wheelchair as well as on one's knees. The patio and garden should be planned with an eye to the ease with which they can be cared for by the residents. These areas should be accessible to wheelchair patients, crutch walkers, and occasionally the completely bedridden.

Porches were traditionally favorite spots for relaxation and good vantage points from which to view activities. In many respects the modern terrace, with or without roof, has replaced the porch, and has retained many of its advantages.

Library

The library should be provided with comfortable chairs and tables, plenty of shelf space, good lighting, and extra storage space. Above all, the library should be used for "living" books and periodicals rather than as a place into which is emptied the refuse of ancient attics and no longer wanted collections. Thirty feet of the "five-foot shelf" does not make a good library. If an interested resident takes charge of the library, this room can be one of the most active in the whole home—and at moderate expense.

Part of the library should be devoted to a portable section so that books and periodicals can be taken to the bedridden. Regular rounds should be made with fresh material appealing to individual tastes. "Talking" books for the blind, and "ceiling" books for special disability cases can be an important part of the library.

Snack bar and gift shop

The snack bar and gift shop should be arranged to supply the simple needs and desires of residents and visitors. It should be close to the entrance of the home, but also easily accessible to the residents.

The stock on hand should be related to the resources made available by the building location. If the home is near a shopping area, for example, it will not be necessary to include many of the items that a gift shop for a home in a rural setting would require. This shop should

also be used to sell items made by the residents in the crafts program and in occupational therapy.

Personnel for the operation of these areas can be drawn from the resident self-government program (if there is one). Through the use of residents' skills, and close interest and supervision by the administrator, it is not too farfetched to expect a profit, with the funds to be used for some special purpose commonly agreed upon.

The food sold at the snack bar should be limited to snacks and should never substitute for regular meals. Close observation by the medical director is necessary to prevent evasion of special diets, particularly by diabetics.

Recreation facilities

The areas in which recreation programs are conducted should be planned in cooperation with the occupational therapy department. However, the emphasis should always be on recreation and joy in living and doing.

It is impossible to list every facility that can be used in these programs. The range is limited only by the imagination of those entrusted with their establishment, the desires of the residents themselves, and of course, available funds. The rooms used for recreation should be flexible enough to meet changing needs and tastes. Numerous electrical outlets, plumbing fixtures, simple tables and chairs, plenty of storage space —all these should be available. Soundproofing will avoid many headaches, both literally and figuratively.

The space for the crafts program should include areas for carpentry, ceramics, painting, printing, knitting and crocheting, leather work, bookbinding, photography, pottery, enamel on copper, and the like.

A soundproof music room with a good high fidelity system will provide hours of pleasure for the residents. Earphones for private listening, storage space for records and tapes, comfortable furniture, and pleasing decoration can make for

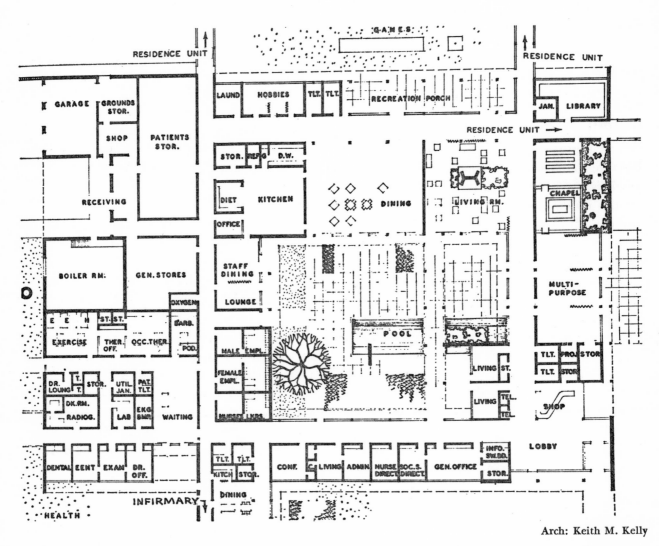

Arch: Keith M. Kelly

A central courtyard constitutes the main plan element around which all the congregate functions are gathered. The entrance lobby is somewhat divorced from the living area, but is well related to administration and the multipurpose room. This relationship is helpful when outside organizations use the home for meetings or entertainment. An altar leads on one side to a small, intimate chapel with independent access, and on the other to the multipurpose room.

All traffic to the residence units passes by the open sides of the living area and thereby serves to enliven it. It is also well related to the central courtyard and to the dining area. Hobby and library areas are well located, as are the small living rooms (near the entrance) for private entertainment.

a most popular spot. It should be possible to connect the sound equipment in the music room to the general intercom system, to provide concerts for the bed bound.

Billiard and game rooms are desirable if space and funds permit.

Sheltered workshop

In larger institutions it may be possible to develop a program of paid work, and if such a program is anticipated space must be provided for it. When conducted with the cooperation of the medical staff and coordinated by the occupational therapist, the earning incentive of work in the sheltered workshop can make for a better balance in congregate living.

Conclusion

The foregoing may sound elaborate and complex. Actually, the services proposed can be made to fit into any plan. The importance of each aspect—dining room, living room, chapel, recreation—should be weighed in relation to the total plan for a home for the aged. Some aspects may receive less emphasis than others, but provision should be made for all of them as well as for future expansion and development.

If the home is to be a place in which to live, it must provide services that enable the individual to live his years to the full—with privacy as desired, but always with the possibility of the warm companionship of his fellow man.

5: The Residence Unit and Room

By Whitney R. Smith, AIA
Smith and Williams, Architects & Site Planners, Pasadena, California

The resident's own room and the residence unit of which it is a part will largely determine the degree to which he feels at home in a congregate living situation. It is for this reason that some planners of homes for the aged have preferred to use a series of small private dwellings, with all their obvious hazards and disadvantages, for groups of eight or ten residents each, rather than to provide a single building for the entire population.

The residence unit

There is no doubt that as the number of residents in each unit increases the possibility of retaining a homelike atmosphere decreases. In the traditional institution with its long, straight corridors, the homelike atmosphere practically vanishes.

For reasons of economy or the need to provide for considerable numbers, most homes must be built to accommodate more than a family-size group, but opinion varies widely on the size of the home that is ideal for economy, efficiency, and the well-being of residents. It is obviously uneconomical to provide many of the services discussed elsewhere in this book for a small group of people. But it is possible, through careful planning and design, to create the feeling of being part of a smaller, more intimate group regardless of the total number of beds in the home.

Thirty is probably the maximum permissible number of residents for any one unit, and since a residence unit may later be converted to an infirmary, twenty may be more desirable for staffing and control.

The people who live in each unit form a sort of family group within the total resident population. Even within the unit the group can be further broken down through the use of short corridors. By this means the resident is given the feeling of living only with those people whose rooms open off his own corridor, rather than with the entire group, as when all the rooms are ranged on either side of a long, straight hall.

Such long corridors, simply because their entire length is visible, are actually more tiring to move about in than corridors of equal length that are visually broken. Devices such as planting boxes or screens of some sort may be used to focus attention and lessen the sensation of length. Changes in wall materials and color, floor patterns, or ceiling fixtures all help to break distance. On the other hand, endlessly winding corridors can be very confusing for some elderly people, and they are difficult for a nurse to control. Overly complicated schemes should therefore be avoided. To reconcile the desirability of short, direct circulation on the one hand, and the dimensions inevitable in a unit housing thirty residents on the other, requires planning skills of a high order.

Each unit should have its own visual identity and should provide easy access to the common rooms. Even though the residents of each unit form a sort of family group within the whole, it

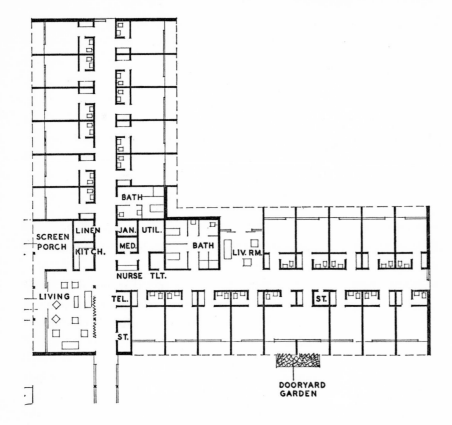

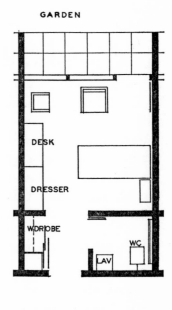

RESIDENCE ROOM
Arch: Keith M. Kelly

This unit plan is a straightforward, logical, and economical arrangement, but the access corridor to the unit should have been placed off the center of the interior corridor for more privacy and a shorter view. Nurses' stations, bathrooms, and utility areas are very conveniently located. The living room, kitchen, and porch are strategically located at the point of maximum activity, and yet do not impede circulation.

The private room is again logical and well done. Using a folding door for the bathroom may create problems for the easily confused resident, who has three types of doors—hinged, folding, and sliding —to contend with. The toilet presents real problems for the wheelchair resident. On the whole, while this is not an inspired plan, there is very little in it to criticize, and much to learn from.

is a rather large family, and every effort must be made to provide relative privacy for small group gatherings. Each unit needs its own small living room, with minimum cooking facilities adjacent, for individual entertaining or for small parties of residents. Some homes provide lockers or refrigerator space or both for the storage of residents' own food to be used for entertaining or for between-meal snacks. Such a practice pre-

sents obvious administrative problems but has the tremendous advantage of giving residents a sense of independence and self-direction.

Design

Individual residence rooms dictate, by their size, shape, and juxtaposition, the over-all design and structural pattern of the residence unit. The actual design relationship of the residence rooms to each other and to the other functions and buildings of the institutional group may take many forms—widely dispersed with wide, landscaped expanses; grouped in clusters with smaller landscaped courts; or very compact and multistoried, for example.

In multistory buildings, a floor or wing may become the residence unit, and the same considerations apply as to single-story buildings. Although multistory buildings are usually considered only when land costs are high, the design possibility of raising all the residence rooms above the first floor and reserving the entire ground area for communal, recreational, educational, and service functions is an interesting one.

The residence room

The individual residence room constitutes the final retreat from group living; freedom of individual expression within each room is therefore vital. Here, particularly, is it important to know as much as possible about the people who will occupy the rooms. Their state of health and mobility, cultural interests, national and occupational backgrounds, and traditions—all will influence the planning of the individual room and its furnishings.

From the standpoint of construction economy, it is probable that room layouts will be almost identical except for location and orientation. It is, therefore, primarily in the area of furniture selection and placement, wall covering and color, upholstery, drapes, bedspreads, and the like that maximum personal choice may be demonstrated.

A room planned so that several furniture arrangements may be made is better than one planned for just one or two, because the resident is free to rearrange the furniture from time to time, and because a minimum number of rooms will have the same appearance. This variety will help considerably in eliminating a hotel-like atmosphere.

Within some limits, it would seem that the room occupant should be able to bring along and use his own furniture, television and radio sets, and personal possessions. The limits would exclude unsafe furniture, torn or loose rugs, loud musical instruments, and the like.

The furniture a resident may wish to bring into a home is often so heavy, clumsy, and generally unsuitable, that the management must forbid its use. The home must therefore have furniture available that will better suit the purpose—well-made, comfortable, and light enough to be moved easily. In certain climates, some of the furniture should be usable out-of-doors.

Furniture should be tested to ensure that it is convenient for older people to sit in and arise from, a feature not always attainable in some of the lower and armless types of chairs. Much of today's furniture meets these standards. The right furnishings can add to comfort, flexibility, appearance, safety, and enjoyment without adding to cost.

As eyes become older, more light is required. Some experts point out that for corresponding situations two to three times the amount of light normally required is desirable for older people. Fortunately, great improvements are being made in artificial lighting systems. The single bare lamp with its glare and contrasting shadows is no longer considered adequate for reading, sewing, and similar work. The "floor lamp" is not much better.

One effective device is a luminous ceiling to be used over a portion of the resident's room—in effect, a corrugated or otherwise deformed plastic sheet that glows with relatively low intensity and spreads a uniform, high-intensity, shadowless light over a wide area. Less expensive fixtures that provide nearly the same effect are commonly used in new school classrooms today. They employ a silver bowl lamp, concentric metal rings, and use the entire ceiling as a light reflector.

The need to consider furnishings in relation to residents' capabilities as the room design is

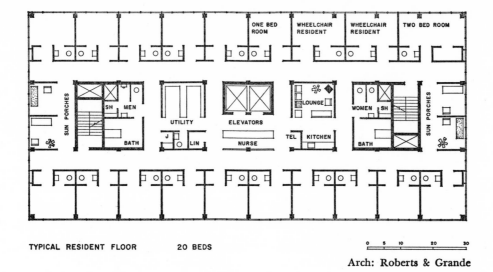

TYPICAL RESIDENT FLOOR   20 BEDS

Arch: Roberts & Grande

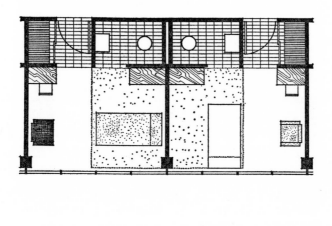

Arch: Roberts & Grande

The relative discipline and rigidity imposed when planning a high-rise building are evident in this plan when compared to some of the other single-story schemes. One can only hope that its institutional character would be effectively subdued by subtle detailing and careful use of materials, color, and lighting. Obvious faults such as the lack of clearance in front of the elevators and the wasteful multiplicity of access between the main corridors are not inherent in such a plan.

The rooms themselves are well laid out and spacious. While the use of a carpet to delineate the sleeping and living areas might be dangerous, the objective is excellent. As simple an idea as a change in floor color or of wall material or even of ceiling height might help in achieving such an effect.

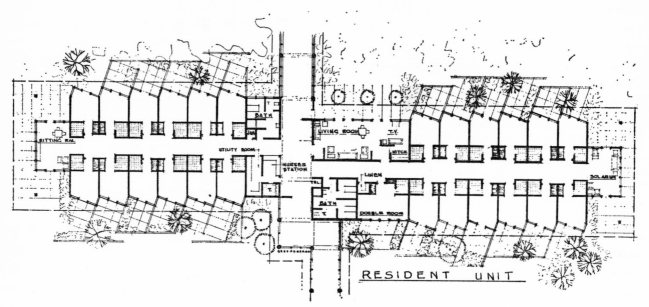

RESIDENT UNIT

Arch: Gould & Leaf

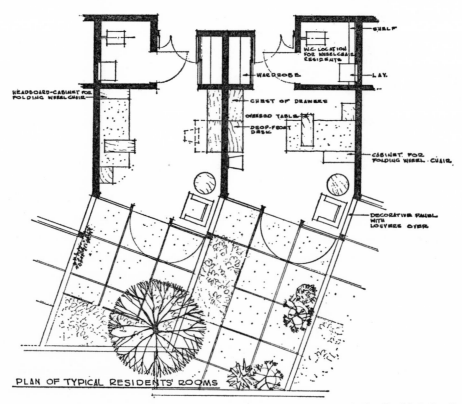

PLAN OF TYPICAL RESIDENTS' ROOMS

Arch: Gould & Leaf

being developed cannot be overemphasized. Most residents have disabilities that vary in kind and degree. Some spend most or all of their time in wheelchairs or on crutches, and maneuvering space is required as well as storage space near the bed. To those with faulty vision or unsteady balance, awkward projections on furniture may be hazardous. And, of course, there are always those relatively able-bodied residents—who want to take care of their rooms, make their beds, and generally lead independent lives—for whom housekeeping should be made as easy as possible.

The type of window used should be easy to control from a wheelchair or by someone with reduced strength and flexibility in arms or hands. Too wide a sill might prevent a resident in a wheelchair or on crutches from reaching the window controls. Poorly fitting sash and down drafts must be avoided, since residents often like to sit at a window. Window sills should be low enough to permit a view outside when the occupant of the room is lying in bed. Drapes and blinds at windows should be easy to operate with a minimum of agility and strength. The amount of glass at the outside wall is a matter of individual design.

Room size

In general, the room size should be large enough for the occupant to express some individuality. Beyond this point the optimum size of the room depends to a considerable degree on the extent of the communal facilities offered by the institution. Obviously, a larger residence room would be required in a home providing no such facilities.

It is probably a sound idea to make every room large enough for two people, so that two beds may be provided if the situation demands. There are several reasons why this provision is advisable. It would allow any room (rather than a smaller, fixed number of rooms) to be used for two people. It allows for assignment of any room to either a single person or a couple. And even single occupants may need a companion or nurse at some time, or may wish to have overnight guests.

It is suggested also that, if possible, all rooms conform in size, shape, and finishes to hospital standards. Naturally, some objections due to increased costs arise, but there are also distinct advantages to this scheme. First, most of the hospital requirements—wider halls, wider

---

Several devices have been employed in this unit plan to reduce its apparent size and scale and to add interest. Most noticeable is the way the corridors are jogged to avoid needlessly long vistas. The nurses' station also gains in visual control but care would have to be exercised to avoid overemphasis of the supervisory aspect. Projecting screens in the main connecting corridor near the nurses' station also help to reduce apparent size by providing strong points of interest.

Corridors within the unit are helped considerably by recessing each pair of doors from the main corridor partitions. Sitting rooms at either end of the unit provide very desirable small-scale arrangements for conver-

sation and the like, but could have been reduced to half their present size without diminishing their value.

The individual rooms are easy to furnish, having four interior corners free of circulation. By canting the exterior wall, extra living space has been achieved; but even better, the return of the window should give a sense of spaciousness hard to achieve otherwise. Whether to fence the individual gardens outside each room would depend on the wish of the resident for a distant or intimate view from his window. The toilets are not well planned for wheelchair use. The use of double-leaf doors at the corridors is somewhat questionable.

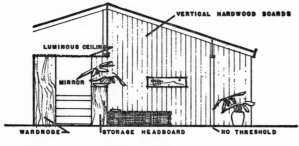

INTERIOR RESIDENT UNIT

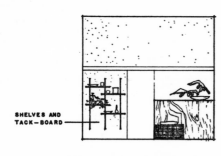

INTERIOR RESIDENT UNIT

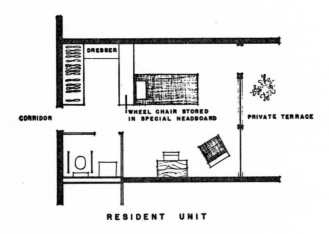

RESIDENT UNIT

Arch: Smith & William

This room would be a delightful place to live in. It reflects much of the homelike character that is to be found in the best contemporary residential designs. The dressing area, with its luminous ceiling—actually separate but visually a part of the room— would have a special appeal for women. The flower and knickknack shelves contrasting with the vertical boards and sloping ceiling produce the very opposite of the institutional look. The plan allows many furniture arrangements to suit individual tastes, and will therefore delight the person who likes to change things around once every six weeks.

personal care may be administered to those not actually ill or infirm but who may need some help with a difficult task.

There is even a special kind of hospital bed that looks like a normal bed when lowered. Although more expensive than regular beds, these would prove most helpful in avoiding an institutional appearance. The units should not look like hospital rooms.

When planning a home, it is impossible to predict how many residents will need bed care periodically or permanently. Therefore, "every residence room to meet minimum hospital standards" might prove a profitable motto for some homes.

Baths and toilets

Tubs and showers should probably be grouped within the residence units, with a supervising nurse or attendant available. Many older people need help with bathing, and it therefore seems more economical as well as safer to group these facilities.

On the other hand, a private toilet with a lavatory and water closet for each room is desirable from many standpoints. A toilet shared between two rooms always presents the problem of occupants forgetting to lock or unlock doors, apart from the likelihood of one person needing it while another is using it. A homelike atmos-

doors, increased fire protection, more easily cleaned materials—yield greater safety, lower insurance costs, and lower maintenance costs. The principal advantage, however, is flexibility, for if rooms conform to hospital standards nursing care may be provided in every room, and phere is reduced by even such limited sharing of facilities and disappears entirely when toilets are grouped centrally for common use.

Wheelchair access head on to the water closet and to the lavatory is essential, although side access to the water closet is occasionally used when the arms of the wheelchair are removable. It is best if the lavatory is built into a counter, the bottom of which should clear the top of the arm rests of a wheelchair. The lavatory bowl and its supporting hardware should fit between the arm rests. Combination faucets (never spring faucets) should be used. Open shelves for toilet articles and a mirror mounted for use from a wheelchair should be provided.

The width and placement of the doorway, the kind of door (hinged or sliding), and its hardware, knobs or handles—all should also be planned for wheelchair use. The cost of a room so planned is slightly above the minimum required for ambulant residents only, but maximum flexibility is assured for the future.

Atmosphere

The degree to which the residence unit and the individual rooms approach a homelike atmosphere is a direct gauge of the architect's skill and understanding. When he is supported by a sponsoring group whose policies and vision meet the challenge of the many problems involved, the resulting home will be a very pleasant and rewarding place to live in.

6: Health Needs

By Dr. Frederic D. Zeman, M.D., F.A.C.P.
Chief of Medical Services, the Home for Aged and Infirm Hebrews, New York

Until recently, institutions for the aged in this country have, for the most part, reflected the apathy of both physicians and the general public. The old-fashioned "home for the aged," whether under voluntary or public sponsorship, was satisfied to supply bed and board to its residents, who were assumed to be healthy enough so that only occasional medical care would be needed.

Today, as a result of more intensive study of the medical and social problems of older men and women, the home for the aged has relinquished its passive attitudes, and has developed active programs of prevention and treatment to such a point that it has come to be regarded as an intermediate medical facility. Maintaining the same high standards of medical, nursing, and social service practice as the general hospital for chronic diseases, the home for the aged is devoting itself more and more to the active care of the handicapped and disabled aged.

The modern home for the aged is differentiated from the general hospital in that, among other things, it admits residents for life and imposes certain specific limitations in the kind of care offered. Surgical cases as well as those requiring elaborate diagnostic or therapeutic procedures are temporarily transferred to the general hospital. By this means, maintenance and duplication of expensive ancillary services are avoided and costs are reduced.

It is obvious that while certain medical installations are necessary in a home for the aged, they will be far less complex than those of a general hospital. On the other hand, far more attention must be paid to recreational and occupational therapy areas, to the provision of closet space in the rooms, to safety measures, to the creation of a relaxed, congenial atmosphere, and to the development of flexible plans to take care of the ever-changing requirements of the residents.

Whether homes for the aged should be located in separate buildings on the grounds of a general hospital is a question that has been much debated. Hospital administrators favor such a proposal because of: the ready availability of medical care and diagnostic facilities; reduced costs, for example, in laundry and heating installations; and greater ease in management. This writer willingly admits that these are important considerations, but insists that where this plan has been followed the old people have come off second-best in the competition for medical attention. The pressing demands of the critically ill lead to the neglect of the old people, who, in the minds of hospital staffs, professional and nonprofessional, present not only uninteresting but often disturbing problems.

Stephen Paget, in discussing hospitals, spoke of the characteristic "genius loci." The spirit of a home for the aged is totally different from that of a general hospital. The whole tempo is slower, with patient turnover low, so that the staff comes to know the residents intimately, and to participate happily in the unending battle against encroaching and accumulating years.

The modern home for the aged is truly "patient-centered," not "disease-centered," as is the

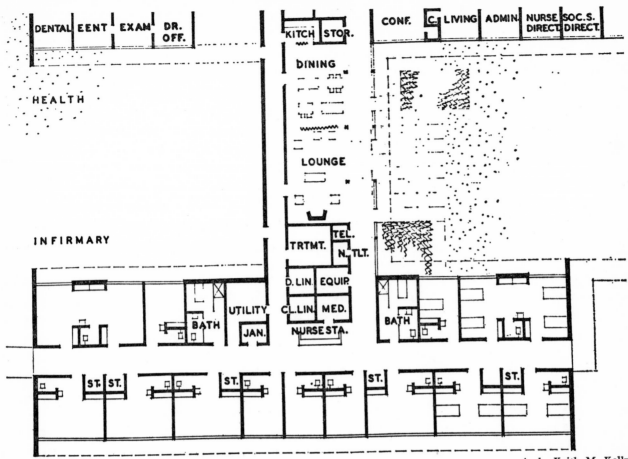

Arch: Keith M. Kelly

This infirmary plan is generally well laid out for nursing. The nurses' station is centrally located for equal access to both ends of the corridor, and controls all traffic entering or leaving the unit. However, there is no direct control of the lounge-dining area; such control is desirable because of the uncertain habits of some of the ambulant residents. Under these circumstances there should be no fireplace in the lounge, and even with direct visual control, the hazard is probably not justifiable. Similarly, there should be no

access from the lounge to the outside terrace without positive means of control, because of the hazards involved.

The arrangement of the utility and linen rooms does not reflect a knowledge of the nurses' work pattern. In this and most other plans for infirmaries, much more study and research into hospital planning is necessary. The individual rooms are well laid out except for the four-bed ward, which is oversized. Baths, toilets, and showers are well planned and grouped.

hospital. The physician entering the independently located and managed home for the aged automatically concentrates his thinking and his activities on the problems of old age, free from the distractions so common in general hospitals.

Detailed discussions of such matters as location, size, recreation, facilities, and the like are

reserved for other parts of this book. It should be pointed out, however, that many of these topics have a significant bearing on the health of the resident, and that the doctor should be interested in all aspects of the building plan, not just the infirmary and other medical facilities.

The physician recognizes that a home for the aged should be near former residences and convenient for visits from friends and relatives; that a garden has a therapeutic value; that large installations lose the personal intimate touch essential in maintaining human values; and that all of these factors may affect the physical and mental health of the residents.

With these considerations in mind the architect should understand the great interest of the physician both in the larger aspects and in the details of the plans, and his keen desire to enter into a productive collaboration. Since ease and comfort in living form so large a part of the psychotherapeutic function of an institution, the medical consultants should think in terms of mental health, and show as much concern for proper decoration and lighting as for the plumbing and heating arrangements.

In planning the ratio of beds for the severely handicapped or acutely ill to those for ambulatory patients with less severe disabilities, the admissions policy of the organization must be taken into consideration. Even though an effort be made to screen out individuals needing maximum care, time will surely cause many residents to change from ambulatory to bed bound. At least half the bed capacity may eventually be devoted to those needing active medical or nursing care, or both, and appropriate provisions must be made for nursing stations and utility rooms. In a well-planned home of moderate size, residents suffering from minor intercurrent illnesses (those that arise during and may affect other illnesses) can be taken care of in their own rooms.

The medical area

The activities of the medical department of the home should be grouped together and adjacent to the infirmary area for most efficient operation. A sufficient number of offices for resident and attending physicians, as well as for the director of nursing, must be provided. The office of the chief of service should be large enough for staff conferences and small committee meetings. Toilet and lavatory facilities should form part of this office suite.

The medical secretary's office may serve as a record room and may also house a small medical library. In view of the tendency of most libraries to outgrow their facilities, a separate room is desirable, which may double as a conference or committee room. Examining rooms, with adjoining dressing rooms, should be large enough to contain a standard examining table, two or three straight chairs, and a small table for instruments, and to allow for physician, nurse, and patient to move about freely.

Separate offices, or workrooms, must be provided for the dentist and the podiatrist. A laboratory equipped with a chemical hood, and with gas, electricity, and compressed air and suction outlets, is essential for precise clinical studies. A small room for electrocardiographic and basal metabolism studies is also needed. Space for storage of drugs is essential.

Diagnostic X-ray equipment should be installed in the medical area. One room is required for equipment and another, smaller one as an office and viewing room for the roentgenologist. A toilet should be provided close to the X-ray room for patients who have had diagnostic barium meals.

Extra rooms suitable for future conversion into research laboratories often prove very useful to the medical staff.

The rehabilitation and physical medicine equipment may be placed in the medical area, or should perhaps be close to the infirmary to facilitate the movement of patients. The physical therapy room should provide exercise facilities, such as parallel bars, and a variety of mechanical devices, as well as whirlpool baths for arms and legs. Small cubicles should be available for massage tables and for electrotherapeutic devices. The design of rehabilitation facilities for hospitals has been thoroughly developed, and much of the material on this subject is highly applicable to homes for the aged.

The infirmary area

If the home's residents are to require active medical and nursing care for long-term or acute intercurrent illnesses, the infirmary installation should approach general hospital specifications. Units of two beds are preferred, although some four-bed units are permissible in order to facilitate the work of the nursing staff. Each bed must have a bed light and call bell. Doors to single or two-bed units must have windows to allow quick inspection by passing nurses. Nurses' stations and utility rooms must be provided. Each floor must have one or two single-bed units near the nurses' stations for the moribund or noisy patient. A bedpan flushing attachment should be provided at each water closet.

Nursing stations must be provided with desks, chart racks, and storage closets for supplies and equipment. Glass-fronted cupboards are sufficient for the ordinary drugs in frequent use, but a locked compartment must be provided for the supply of narcotics, however small.

The patients' rooms should be large enough to allow the easy circulation of nurses and orderlies as well as bulky equipment such as oxygen tents and orthopedic appliances. Closet space and locks should be more liberally provided than in a general hospital, because the patients' stays are much more prolonged and they may bring along a large quantity of clothing and other possessions.

Provision of storage space for wheelchairs in the patients' rooms and infirmary areas is often omitted or overlooked. Wheelchairs left standing about in hallways are accident hazards and unsightly as well.

Separate paths of circulation should be planned to prevent business people, or visitors to the healthy residents, encroaching on the area for the sick, and to separate streams of visitors to different parts of the building. The medical offices, examining rooms, and infirmary must all be accorded privacy. Sitting rooms for patients awaiting examination, and for visitors to the infirmary area, help to avoid congestion in hallways and reduce noise.

In large institutions (over 200 beds) a morgue and autopsy room should be inconspicuously located outside the infirmary area, but should be easily accessible so as to avoid transporting bodies for long distances and traversing public halls.

Occupational therapy

The varied pursuits that constitute occupational therapy require a small suite of rooms, each devoted to one or more special activities such as woodworking, basket weaving, ceramics, leather crafts, painting, fabric weaving, and bandage rolling. An office for the therapist is needed, as well as display cases for the products made. These cases should be located both in the occupational therapy area and at the main entrance of the home. The rooms must be large enough to accommodate six to eight men and women, working independently, but enjoying the benefits of group effort.

7: Administration and Staff Facilities

By Edith S. Alt
Director, Project on Standards of Care for Older People in Institutions, National Committee on
   the Aging

The first impression of the reception and administrative offices of a home for the aged will deeply affect the older person seeking residential care, his relatives or friends, and others visiting or working in the home.

As the visitor or resident travels from one office to another he will react to the atmosphere of the home as he sees it reflected in the physical plant, equipment, furnishings, and surroundings, and as he feels it in the manner and attitude of the personnel.

Serenity, friendliness, and efficiency, all necessary components in the administration of a home, can be maintained more readily if the environment is specifically planned to enhance them. Reception and waiting rooms and offices should reflect the knowledge that frequent sensitive discussions, and, sometimes, difficult decisions will take place there.

Similar consideration for the physical handicaps of old age must be given when planning the administrative units. A particular problem here is the need to provide offices with sufficient privacy for interviewing purposes, not only to aid the older people in communication, but to maintain serenity in a group living situation. Some persons with hearing difficulties require others to talk loudly or even to shout; some frightened older people will not talk freely about personal matters in a strange place if they feel others might overhear them.

The decision to enter the home may have been reached easily and happily, but often the old people applying or their relatives are deeply disturbed about taking this step, and family tension may be at a high pitch—then or at other times, during the resident's stay.

Tension often arises in the course of inquiries about the home, especially when an application for admission is processed, so that it is wise to plan the reception quarters for ample privacy.

Cheerful surroundings, adequate working space, and sufficient privacy are essential working tools.

The heavy emotional strains on the personnel working in these facilities should not be overlooked. Those planning homes should make sure that the appearance and dignity of the working offices add to the staff's own feeling of status. When the value of the administrative and professional staff's work is thus affirmed by the sponsors and trustees, the residents, too, will benefit from feelings of dignity and friendliness.

Reception lobby

The reception lobby should be located at the building entrance. Access to the lobby and movement to other offices should be made as simple as possible for the physically handicapped older person.

The entrance to the lobby should be homelike, welcoming, and attractive; wide enough for a wheelchair or walker; and unencumbered, so that visually handicapped persons can manage without undue embarrassment.

Soundproof private interviewing space near

40

the lobby and reception quarters, as has already been mentioned, is essential. Depending on size and particular requirements, some homes may wish to anticipate future needs and plan for more small private rooms.

Offices for personnel

Offices for the administrator, head nurse, dietitian, social worker, and for all office personnel should be cheerful, comfortable, and appropriate to the specific functions involved.

The number and size of administrative offices depend on several factors, including the size of the home, the type of program to be undertaken, and the extent of growth anticipated. The most important of these considerations is probably the type of program contemplated.

A home for the aged, regardless of size, requires a series of administrative offices for even a minimal program of activities. The institution with but one office—that of the "supervising matron" or "superintendent"—has gone the way of the poor farm. It has been superseded by the modern home, which employs a team of administrative and professional personnel working under the direction of an administrator.

Working space must therefore be provided, at some point near the reception lobby, for the administrator, medical director, social work director, the business offices, records and financial files, information and telephone services, and so on. Offices for other functions may also be located here, depending upon the complexity of the home's program. Chaplains, directors of volunteer services, fund raising or public relations staff—all these might require offices.

It is not intended here to list all personnel who might possibly require separate offices, but rather to point out that many homes do utilize all these services, and provide them with offices that are near each other and also near the reception lobby and conference room. While some homes may not need all these specialized services early in their development, planning

groups should be aware that they are generally present in a well-rounded program.

The number of offices should be determined not only by the present program but by the likelihood of future expansion. Many homes are being increasingly urged by community groups to add more beds and new day-center activities for nonresidents, or to consider interim care (short-stay) residents. Unless the home is planned with the awareness that such pressures are likely because of urgent and increasing demands for service, there is a danger that reception quarters and offices for administrative and professional personnel may become inadequate in a very short time, thus blocking maximum use of the home's plant.

Information center

An information desk should be located near the entrance to the lobby, possibly in a separate room with its own counter facing the lobby. The room may also include the switchboard, if the desk and switchboard may be operated together courteously and efficiently.

Some homes use the information desk for an "in and out" register of visiting doctors, special staff members, and others so that telephone calls and messages can be routed to them.

The information center should be so designed that, when necessary (such as at visiting time or holidays), two persons can work in the space provided—one for the information desk and the other for the switchboard.

In a larger home with heavier traffic it may be preferable to separate the information desk from the switchboard by having two separate offices for these functions. Both are vital to the smooth operation and good reputation of a home; it is foolish to restrict their usefulness by squeezing them into cramped quarters.

Business office

The general business office should house all the financial records and accounts of the home

—including all books, financial reports, statistical reports, corporate accounts, and reports to city and state bodies. The office should also house records of all financial transactions concerning residents—including admission agreements, a record of charges and payments, and any other pertinent matters.

In addition, the business office should maintain an individual folder for each resident with all documents necessary for proper care and legal protection, such as a copy of the admission application and agreement, data on insurance or inheritances, identifying information about relatives and friends, and any instructions for burial.

In some homes personnel records and files are also kept in the business office.

The business manager, chief bookkeeper, or office manager ordinarily takes charge of the general office. There must be enough space to afford him some privacy to carry on his work, and to allow for assistants (whose number will vary with the size of the operation and similar factors), files, and office machines.

Record room

Record rooms with modern filing systems and equipment, and personnel capable of keeping records accurately, confidentially, and efficiently, are essential in a home for the aged. Protection of the residents' interests calls for the utmost care in safeguarding records.

There are additional reasons, though not more compelling, for developing good record systems. These are related to the rapidly growing demand for more and more research into all aspects of care of older persons. Such research, of course, requires thorough and complete records, and an institution in this field without them is at a great disadvantage.

Medical and nursing records are kept separately in most homes, either in the health maintenance department, the infirmary or in the nursing department.

Administrator's office

The administrator of a home for the aged must not only be able to understand the problems of residents, but must also be able to work successfully with a wide variety of individuals and groups—board members, doctors, nurses, social workers, business office personnel, engineers and maintenance workers, local and state health and welfare agencies, and so on.

Service and budget problems, long-range plans as well as immediate crises in the home—all will be brought to the administrator by his department heads for evaluation and solution. Difficulties caused by illness, death, separation, staff shortages, and the like must be met daily without letting staff morale decline lest care to residents suffer.

The administrator's office should help counterbalance the heavy emotional strains of his job. It should have dignity, comfort, privacy, individuality, and warmth. It should not be too different in character from the other offices in the home, so that a visit to this office will never seem "strange" or "different" to a resident or to the staff.

Furnishings and equipment in this office should reflect the same care applied to all the professional and administrative offices. This is not to say that all offices should be alike in size, equipment, furnishings and effects. This sameness would be monotonous and inefficient. However, it should be pointed out that harmonious living may be more readily achieved if we avoid the sharp contrasts exhibited by the living quarters of personnel of different rank in some of the homes of the past. Not only does greater consistency lessen tension among staff, but it may help to promote the feeling of an open home where all rooms are equally attractive, and equally suited to special purposes.

The administrative office should be large enough to accommodate small meetings such as those of board committees or department heads. Even if a conference room is included in the plans, it is important for the administrator to have an office that is always available for meetings on short notice.

Conference room

Every home needs at least one major conference room large enough to hold official meetings, such as those of the trustees or governing board, medical board, residents' council, and staff.

A conference room is also a suitable place in which to hold meetings with outside community groups interested either in the home itself or in the broad problems of older people.

The planning group must determine whether a single conference room is adequate for the home's program or whether more than one is required. Temporary partition devices are used in some homes to allow single conference rooms to handle concurrent meetings.

Because of the high premium currently placed on privacy and the increasing use of professional conferences, it is clear that most homes for the aged will need more small, separate rooms and offices for professional and administrative purposes than were required in the past.

Offices for department heads

Department heads, such as the medical director, nursing director, social work director, head of occupational therapy, nutritionist, and the like require not only private offices but, usually, additional space for other personnel working in association with them. The amount of space necessary depends on many factors, especially the home's stage of development and its program in the particular activity under consideration.

The confidential nature of the work involved, as well as the need for quiet, makes privacy a necessity. Whether a department head is conferring with one of his staff, interviewing a potential resident as part of an intake study, preparing a report on the work of his depart-ment, or trying to help a disturbed resident in adjusting to some personal or intergroup problem, he must maintain the utmost control over his working environment. Sharing the office, even with a secretary, lessens his ability to cope with situations charged with tension.

A detailed description of the functions and responsibilities of various staff members and of the board is included in a publication of the National Committee on Aging: *Standards of Care for Older People in Institutions*; and a study of these will aid in visualizing space needs. The intake process, for example, requires the personal attention of several staff members on several occasions. Guidance and counseling of residents by practically all staff should be available under suitable conditions.

If the home is to expand—into day-center activities, for example—then additional space for social workers, occupational therapists, and similar personnel will be necessary.

Living arrangements for personnel

It is clearly recognized today that the most important attribute of key professional and administrative personnel in a home is the richness of their personal and professional qualifications, rather than their availability at all hours.

Thus, a significant change has taken place. In the past, the "resident matron" or "supervisor" received maintenance as an important part of salary; now, living-in arrangements for administrators, especially of larger homes, are rapidly losing favor.

Those who believe it is more desirable for administrators to live away from the home argue that, among other advantages, this arrangement permits the institution's board a far greater latitude in finding a competent person to fill the post. Many younger men or women, otherwise highly qualified to assume these posts, might decline to bring their own family and children to live in the atmosphere of an institution.

Others who oppose living-in feel that it tends to limit the board's choice of an administrator to persons with more limited emotional and personal resources. On the whole, and especially in newer and larger programs for the aged, practice is tending rapidly toward nonresident administrators. Observers report favorable results, but with some problems.

However desirable nonresidence may prove to be for the mental health of the administrator and key staff, it is nevertheless true that a certain gap in coverage is created. This gap must be met.

When the administrator and other key personnel do not live in, provision must always be made to ensure that a senior staff member, who can take responsibility in case of an emergency, is present at night. Some rooms must be kept available for use as daytime rest rooms for the key staff, or for emergency overnight stays. Such guest rooms may also be used occasionally upon the visit of student observers or others interested in the home.

Not all homes are ready for nonresident administrators. Some may be located in a region where nonresidence is impractical for various reasons—because it may not be possible for the administrator to find suitable quarters at a nominal cost, for example. Other homes may provide excellent residential arrangements for the administrator in a building quite apart from the home and offering ample privacy for himself and his family.

If the decision is made that the administrator should live in the home, then it must be clearly understood that the person to be selected for the post should be the most competent candidate under consideration, and not merely one who can be counted upon to be available at all times.

Staff quarters

There is an increasing desire on the part of institutional personnel for freedom in their personal lives, and other institutions like hos-

pitals have had to adapt to this trend. On the other hand, it is obvious that the safety and care of older people would be jeopardized if all the staff of a home for the aged lived outside the home.

Provision of emergency overnight rooms and daytime rest rooms has been mentioned earlier. These must be available to personnel who live out so that residents will not be deprived of care or endangered because of an emergency, or because the home is located some distance from a city or from transportation facilities. Naturally, it is assumed that adequate staffing will make emergencies rare.

To meet changing developments without undue waste or anxiety, planning for maximum flexibility in staff quarters is essential.

A children's institution, for example, has devised a series of room arrangements to make it possible to have units that can house couples without children, couples with children, or single persons sharing a bathroom. This flexibility is achieved by developing units of four-room apartments with two bathrooms. These units can be assigned to a family with two children, divided by assigning a couple with one child to three rooms with one bath and using the other room and bath for a single person, or split between two couples, each having a two-room and bath apartment.

In older buildings the opportunity for this degree of flexibility may not always be present, but there is every reason to search for newer ways to meet such problems.

Wherever practical, it is desirable to build staff quarters away from the main buildings that house residents. This arrangement will contribute to the staff's feeling of freedom for personal activities, which is such an important element in any group living situation.

The achievement of a well-coordinated, meaningful, and harmonious institutional program for older people is rooted in the competence and attitudes of the personnel who work with and care for them. Only by helping this staff to feel genuinely appreciated can the most desirable level of service be attained.

The leadership, imagination, and courage required of the administrator and his key staff to develop a creative program must be supported by a sponsoring group who will, as a minimum, assure the working environment essential to the success of this kind of effort.

8: Service and Mechanical Facilities

By August F. Hoenack
Chief, Architectural and Engineering Branch, Division of Hospital and Medical Facilities, U.S.
Public Health Service

The various service functions of the home for the aged are, in many ways, largely responsible for its efficient operation, for the working conditions of the staff, and most important of all, for the comfort and safety of the residents. These functions must be carried out in as unobtrusive a manner as possible.

For example, the residents may be pleasantly made aware, at meal times, that a kitchen is in the building, but this impression should not be unpleasantly reinforced by the sight of garbage cans in the service yard. All service facilities influence the attitude of residents toward their new home.

Adequate materials and supplies must be kept where needed, in the quantities required, and in good repair. It should be possible to repair the electrical system and the plumbing and other mechanical services without having to shut down extensive portions of these systems and cause inconvenience to residents and staff.

The architect with these considerations in mind can contribute immeasurably, through his design, to the comfort and well-being of individuals who are thrust into a situation that is fraught with problems of social and emotional adjustment. The architect's understanding, sensitivity, and skill must be directed toward achieving a wholesome integration of these essential services with the other activities of the home.

The extent of these services from the standpoint of space and personnel required must vary with the size of the home. However, the essential functions and the personnel responsibilities involved are substantially the same for a small home as for a very large one.

Service approaches

The use of the service entrance and driveway should in no way detract from the safe and pleasant use of the grounds. The elderly should be discouraged from walking in the service driveway through provision of adequate sidewalks in adjacent areas and appropriate arrangement of shrubbery. If the service drive is completely separate from the main entrance drive, there is less likelihood of parked passenger cars interfering with the movements of delivery trucks.

Service entrance

Enclosed space should be provided at the service entrance for the storage of garbage and trash waiting to be picked up, and for supplies and food that have been delivered but have not yet been brought to either central stores or the kitchen. In this way the delivery platform need not be an eye-offending catch-all for these items.

One service entrance that is used both for receiving stores and by employees may suffice, but it is better for employee morale if a separate entrance is provided for them.

The vestibule should be large enough to

allow for opening boxes and crates, checking specifications against purchase orders, and weighing foodstuffs. A large scale, possibly a built-in floor model, should be in a convenient location. An office with a large window opening on this vestibule should be provided for the storekeeper. This office should contain files for purchase orders, requisitions, catalogues, and other records and data that may be his responsibility. It should also, if possible, be connected with the general storage room.

Regardless of the size of the institution, it is desirable that responsibility for the receiving and distribution of all supplies be vested in one person. However, in the small home there may not be sufficient activity connected with this function to occupy the full time of one person, and this responsibility may be combined with that of housekeeping.

Central stores

The amount of space needed for central storage depends on the location of the home, the buying practices of the administration, and the available local sources of supply. Generally, a minimum of 10 sq. ft. per resident should be provided. This allowance is required for the storage of household and nursing supplies, bulk food and canned goods, china, furniture, and the like.

All the storage space should be located in one part of the building near the service entrance. The utilization of various left-over spaces throughout the building makes it very difficult to control inventory and maintain a single responsibility for supplies, and could lead to larger investments in inventory than would otherwise be necessary. However, it is desirable to divide the central storage area into separate, contiguous spaces for furniture, bulk food, and household supplies.

All of the space must be dry and well ventilated and lighted. The location of the lighting system should be planned in conjunction with that of the shelving so that enough light is available where it is needed. Adjustable shelving should be provided in various depths. Platforms are needed for the storage of bulk food, and racks for the storage of mattresses, springs, and bed ends.

This area may also include trunk storage space for individual belongings in the residence units, where they would be more easily accessible. (Each resident requires a minimum of 15 sq. ft. of such storage space.) Racks to hold the trunks should be provided for maximum accessibility.

Storage space for lawn mowers and other grounds maintenance equipment can be located anywhere convenient to the grounds where a direct outside entrance is available. A garage, for example (if one is provided), may house this space. If the grounds are extensive enough, it would be desirable to combine the garage and the grounds maintenance equipment in a separate building. Garden furniture, as well, could be stored in such a building during the winter months, although during the summer it could be protected from inclement weather in a shed (which need not be unattractive), built for the purpose near by.

Kitchen

The kitchen of a home for the aged should differ little from any other kitchen serving the same number of people. Yet there are a few factors that may influence the design and kinds of equipment provided. For example, since the diners are older people, less fried food may be served than normally. The extent to which the menu will be varied, and the number of staff to be fed must also be considered. There should usually be one fixed menu for each meal, except of course for those residents requiring special diets.

The basic kitchen areas are those set aside for food storage and refrigeration, preparation, cooking, serving, and dishwashing. These areas should be arranged to provide a flow of the food materials from storage to serving, so that

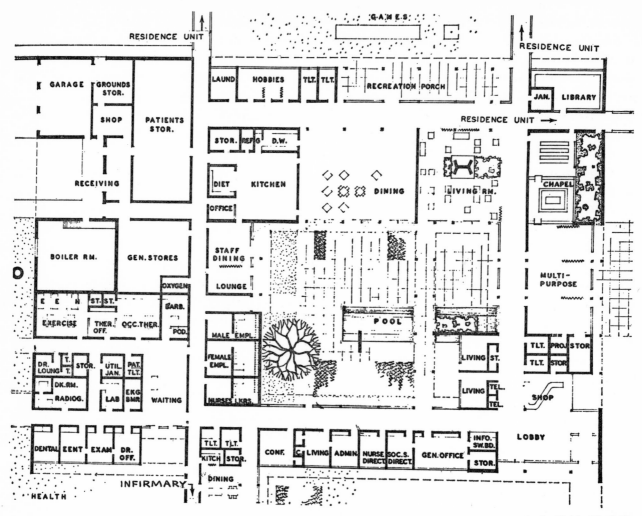

Arch: Keith M. Kelly

In this plan the service elements have been grouped together on the main floor of the home; this arrangement makes for easy control of deliveries, storage, and dispatching with no elevatoring problems. Central location of service causing minimum interference with residence units is unusually well carried out. Circulation from the kitchen to the main and staff dining areas, the infirmary and the residence units is direct, although some conflict and cross traffic are involved in the last two areas. This conflict is somewhat mitigated because normal traffic to the main dining area and to and from the health facilities will be timed to avoid the serving of meals and perhaps the return of dirty dishes.

Kitchen, staff dining, and locker facilities are split from the remainder of the services by a main traffic artery that must be kept open for resident traffic to the health unit from at least one of the residence units. Delivery to the kitchen, which is largely on a daily basis, is not direct. Although the interference is minor, it could be virtually eliminated by relocating the kitchen entrance. Windows for the kitchen are easy to provide here, and their omission is hard to justify. The kitchen proper appears to be much too small for the number of meals to be prepared, and further development of the plan would undoubtedly require some major reorganization of refrigerator space and the like. The residents' laundry is not well located.

no area interferes with the function of another.

Storage　　Bulk dry and canned foods are brought from central stores to the kitchen day stores; and meat, dairy products, and vegetables are brought from the service entrance to refrigerators. In large homes a separate kitchen receiving door for fresh foods may be desirable.

The size of the home will also determine whether reach-in or walk-in refrigerators should be used. The trend toward using more precut meats and prepared vegetables tends to reduce somewhat the required size of refrigerators. Including deep-freeze storage, approximately 1.25 cu. ft. of refrigerator space per person served will generally be necessary. Today, frozen meats and vegetables are being used by institutions more than formerly. The extent to which the total refrigeration space should consist of deep-freeze units depends on the policy of the home. If it is large enough for walk-in boxes, the deep-freeze units should be built inside them.

Preparation　　From storage, raw vegetables are brought to the preparation area to be peeled, cleaned, and prepared for cooking or made up into salads. In large homes where meat is bought in carcass size, a separate meat preparation area is required.

Cooking　　From the preparation area the flow of food is to the cooking area. Here the size of steamers, kettles, boilers, ranges, and the like depends on both the size of the institution and the kinds of menus decided upon.

Baking　　Although it is usually cheaper to buy bread than to bake it, a bakery is useful for cakes, hot breads, and some desserts. Usually, in small homes, no separate baking unit is provided, since the ovens beneath the range will ordinarily serve the purpose. However, if menus are to include a number of baked desserts, cakes, and hot breads, a separate area for baking may be necessary, unless the baking is done very early, before the cook starts work.

Serving　　Some kitchen system should be established for providing tray service to infir-mary patients or others unable to eat in the dining room. The simplest method is to use an open tray cart on which the trays may be set up; the plates are then filled from a steam table and the hot food is covered. Although the food will not be kept warm for long, this system can be satisfactorily used for a small home if it is well organized.

If there are many patients to be served, one of the food distribution systems designed to keep food warm may be considered. Some of these require special carts with heated and refrigerated sections for hot and cold dishes. Others use special, preheated, insulated dishes. These systems are advantageous from the standpoint of planning, since with them the distance between kitchen and patient, and the time lag between placing food on the tray and serving it, are not critical factors.

Of course, most of the residents will be served in the dining room, and the dishes for each dining table filled from the steam table in the serving area of the kitchen.

Dishwashing　　The dishwashing area should be near the tray loading or serving area. It should preferably be separated from the kitchen by a partition, and so arranged that the person scraping plates and loading the dishwasher cannot also handle the clean dishes. The room should be well ventilated by means of a ventilating hood placed over the dishwasher. The walls should be tile or some other easily cleaned surface.

Garbage　　It is common practice today, if local sewer, regulations permit, to install garbage disposal units at food preparation and dishwashing areas. The disposal units eliminate the need for garbage refrigeration, large garbage cans, can storage space, can washing areas, and the labor involved in moving and washing the cans. Such units ensure better sanitary conditions in the food preparation areas.

Trash, including cans and cartons from the food preparation area, and other refuse from all areas of the home, may be disposed of by

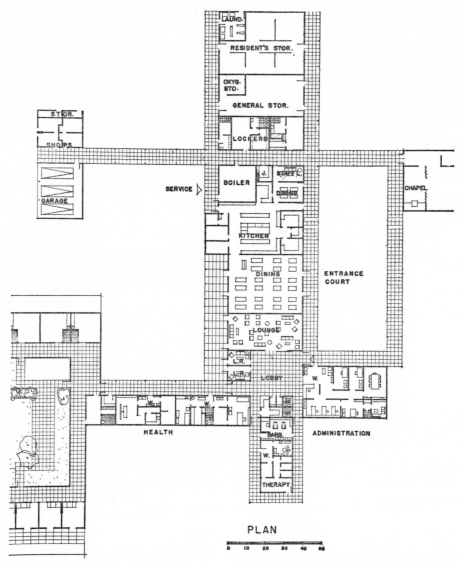

PLAN

0   10   20   30   40   50

Arch: Adam & Lee

Through the use of exterior corridors, service elements in this plan are compactly and centrally located, and there is little conflict with other functions. The kitchen relates well to the main and staff dining areas and also to delivery. General stores and residents' storage are equally accessible from both the service side and the residents' corridor. Access to employees' lockers is good, and the shops and garage form a logical unit well related to the other service functions.

The possibility of conflict between the service court and the dining terrace does exist, but some judiciously located planting or fences would probably solve the problem.

incineration or public removal contract. The incinerator may be located in the boiler room.

Laundry facilities

Whether a home is to maintain its own laundry or use the services of a commercial laundry is a decision that should be based on an accurate analysis of cost and type of service available from each. Consideration should also be given to arranging for a local hospital laundry to provide service. The final decision should be based on answers to the following questions on the commercial and home laundries:

Commercial laundry

1. Does the commercial laundry have sufficient capacity to handle the additional load and maintain satisfactory pick-up and delivery schedules?

2. Is the equipment modern and well maintained?

3. Does the plant have a reputation for continuity of service?

4. What redress is offered if items are damaged or lost?

5. How much larger inventories of linens must be carried to compensate for losses and delays in laundering?

6. Can a contract price for a definite period of time be secured?

7. What are the prices per pound for various classifications of laundry items, including uniforms?

8. What local competition exists?

Home laundry

1. Will the laundry load be sufficient to warrant full-time home laundry personnel?

2. What is the construction cost of the necessary space for the laundry?

3. What is the installed cost of the laundry equipment?

4. What are the fixed annual charges against the plant? (These usually consist of: interest on the investment; amortization of plant and equipment; maintenance costs; supplies such as soaps and detergents; steam, gas, and electricity; wages of personnel; and administration costs.)

Assuming the services offered by each laundry system are comparable, it should then be possible to determine from the above data whether the financial investment in plant and equipment would be economically sound. The decision should be made as soon as possible, so that if the laundry is to be built as part of the home, space allocation and location within the structure may be determined in the initial planning.

Commercial laundry practice provides some guidance in planning, because the load will closely approximate the family laundry handled by such firms. A portion of the load will consist of personal effects that require marking and hand ironing.

Modern acoustical treatment of surfaces and sound insulation of equipment permit the noise hazard of locating the laundry within the building to be overcome. Ceiling height should be at least 11 ft., and it is necessary to provide enough mechanical ventilation to make conditions for the employees comfortable. There must be an adequate supply of soft, hot water at 180°F.

A high-pressure boiler in the boiler room could serve both the laundry and kitchen equipment. Or, installations utilizing equipment heated by gas or electricity may be employed if high-pressure steam is considered undesirable or unwarranted.

If it is decided to use a commercial laundry service, a small central laundry service area must still be provided. This area may be divided into several rooms: one to accommodate soaking tubs for rinsing out soiled linens from incontinent patients prior to pickup by the commercial laundry; one for storage of normally soiled linens pickup; and another for mending and storing clean linens. This central storage is required (in addition to floor linen closets) because of the necessarily larger linen and supply inventory that commercial laundry service necessitates.

It is important to provide a small laundry room readily accessible to the residents. This room should be equipped with ironing boards, soaking tubs, a household washer and dryer, and clothes lines, for those residents who may wish to launder their own personal clothing.

Electrical and signal systems

The electrical system should be designed to provide ample power not only for lighting but also for the many types of equipment used throughout a home for the aged.

Enough outlets should be provided so that extension cords will not be needed. All base plug receptacles in residence rooms should be located 2 ft. above the floor.

Individual residence rooms need not have ceiling lights, but should have plug outlets switched at the entrance door. Rooms in the infirmary section should have bed lights correctly positioned on the walls. Night lights should be provided in all residence rooms.

Nurses' call systems of the intercommunicating type must be installed at each bed and in bath and toilet rooms of the infirmary section. Provision for this system to be extended to every residence room in the home, should the need arise, should be made by roughing-in during construction. Every residence room, bath, and toilet in the home should have an emergency signaling system that will register room numbers at the nurses' station.

Residence rooms may be wired for telephone outlets and connected to the central switchboard. Public telephones should be conveniently located.

For protection against interruption of electrical service, an emergency power system should be provided in all homes for the aged. The system should be large enough to meet the lighting needs of all exits, exit directional signs, stairs, corridors in patient areas, nursing stations, and passageways used for evacuating the building; and to power fire alarms, the heating system, and the nurses' call system. Sewage lift pumps and similar equipment, if used, should also be connected to the emergency power system.

The source of emergency power may be batteries or generator, or a second, independent utility service. Batteries are capable of supplying power for lighting immediately, but for a limited time only. Generating units do not suffer from this limitation, and the time required for starting is usually only a few seconds. Two utility power services entering the home over widely separate routes from separate generating plants, provide adequate and dependable emergency service under most conditions.

Batteries, generating units, and separate services should comply with the requirements of Article 700 of the National Electrical Code. The emergency service should be connected through an automatic transfer switch, interlocked to prevent normal and emergency services from being connected together.

Water supply and sewage disposal

The water supply should be drawn from a public system if possible. If no public supply exists, the purity of the available source should be checked regularly by the state health department or similar agency.

Regardless of the source of supply, it is important that the pressure at the site be known in order that auxiliary power to deliver the water may be provided if needed. Lack of pressure may require the use of roof storage tanks to serve the upper floors.

The chemical and mineral content of the water should also be known, so that proper piping materials may be selected, and water treatment prescribed (if necessary) to inhibit corrosion of lines and boilers, and to provide satisfactory water for laundering and other use.

Two service lines should be brought into the

buildings from two service mains in the streets (if they are available), so that a constant water supply is assured if one main fails.

Fire hydrants should be provided on or adjacent to the site.

Every effort should be made to obtain a site served by a public sewer system. When a sewage disposal system must be installed, the state health agency should be consulted on its design. Lift stations to meet public sewer elevations, or long lines to connect with a distant existing sewer, are usually less expensive to install and operate than a sewage treatment plant.

If lifts are required to meet sewer elevations, pumps should be installed in duplicate, with an emergency source of power to ensure constant service.

Shower stalls and drinking fountains

Shower stalls should be approximately 4 x 4 ft. and should be equipped with a seat and two shower heads—one for the seated and the other for the normal position—each valved independently. Shower stalls for wheelchair use should have no curb. Toilet rooms and shower stalls should have metal handrails on the walls. Hot water at all fixtures used by residents should be thermostatically controlled so that its temperature cannot exceed 110°F.

Drinking fountains with self-contained cooling units should be located for the convenience of the residents, and should be of the combination type of bubbler and faucet, with the faucet set so that water pitchers may be filled.

Boiler plant

A common failing in many institutional buildings is inadequate allocation of space to the boiler room. An analysis of the heating, cooling, ventilating, hot water storage, and miscellaneous services required must be made prior to the selection of equipment. Not until the type and size of equipment has been determined and space assigned to each piece of equip-

ment can the over-all boiler room space be specified. Economy of operation requires a planned program of maintenance that will not, and often cannot, be achieved unless enough space is provided around each piece of equipment for proper servicing and operation.

The ceiling of the boiler room should be high enough to permit easy accessibility to the top of any piece of equipment. When space over the boiler room is to be occupied, the boiler room ceiling must be insulated to prevent overheating the rooms above.

The boiler room should be well lighted and well ventilated. Provision of enough air supply for efficient combustion of fuel in the boilers is too often overlooked. The old saying that "a hot boiler room is an inefficient boiler room" applies to small as well as large installations.

The boiler room may be located within the main building or be separate. It should be near the service entrance, so that fuel deliveries, replacements, and repairs may be easily made. The boiler stack should be so located, and of sufficient height, that the discharged combustion gases will not constitute a nuisance, and will be remote from ventilation air intakes.

The use of high-pressure steam is optional. It is ordinarily used for the laundry, kitchen, and sterilizers. If air conditioning is installed, high-pressure steam might be used for steam jet or steam absorption type refrigeration equipment that could balance the summer boiler load against the winter load.

The chief objection to high-pressure steam has been the code requirement for a licensed operating engineer to be on duty at all times. However, most code requirements are based on the size of the boiler, and many installations are small enough not to require licensed operators.

If no air conditioning is contemplated, or an electrically operated cooling system is to be used, the steam load for laundry and kitchen would be comparatively small. In any event, since the services requiring high-pressure steam are daytime activities, it is not anticipated that

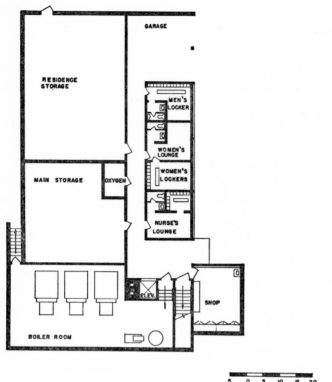

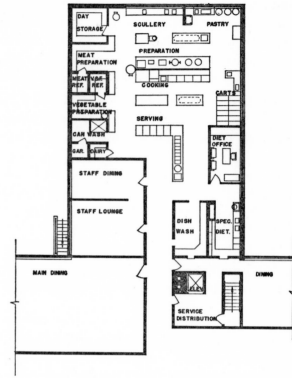

Arch: Steele & Lenker

In this plan, the elements of the service area are split into two levels. Everything related to the preparation and serving of meals is located on the upper level (right). The kitchen is well related to the main and staff dining rooms, although service to and from the main dining room conflicts with traffic to the staff lounge and dining areas. Having to use the elevator or stairs for all daily food deliveries is an inconvenience, and the need for a double entrance elevator could easily have been eliminated.

Storage facilities are placed along one side of the kitchen, feeding logically into preparation and serving, but somewhat remote from the receiving point. Can wash and garbage storage, if used, should be at the lower level off the service entrance. However, these facilities can often be largely eliminated by the use of garbage disposal units strategically located in sinks at such areas as vegetable preparation, meat preparation, and dishwashing.

The lower level (left) contains all storage, boiler, shop, and locker rooms. It is unfortunate that the employees must enter via the loading dock or garage. Boiler room access is very cramped. The shop is well placed for deliveries of material and for access to the home.

supervision would be required during the night.

Snow melting system

If the program of activities encourages walking as a form of exercise, or if there is considerable traffic into and out of the building, a snow removal heating system may be desirable in northern areas.

Such systems are incorporated in walks or exercise areas and are automatically controlled so that they operate only when there is snow on the ground. They are usually hot water systems with pipes embedded in the paving. Antifreeze solution is added for protection against snow-less cold weather. The melting system circuits should be independent of the house heating system. A snow melting system reduces labor costs and very often public liability, if local laws enforce snow removal.

Heating and ventilating

A central heating system should be designed to heat the home to a temperature of about 75°F. for all areas used by the residents. The system should be designed to avoid drafts and cold spots and maintain a constant, uniform temperature. Hot-air heat has the advantage of providing a system that may be utilized for cooling in the summer.

Toilet rooms, kitchens, utility rooms, janitor's closets, and similar areas should have mechanical exhaust ventilation. Inside corridors should have a system of supply including air tempering. Ventilating systems should be designed to avoid drafts, eliminate odors, and help maintain constant uniform temperature. Exhaust ducts should not conduct noise from one room to another.

Air conditioning

While climatic factors determine the ultimate need for air conditioning, accepted standards of comfort make it a virtual necessity for modern buildings in most parts of the country. Because changes in metabolism induced by the aging process make older people very sensitive to extremes of temperature and humidity, air conditioning is particularly important in homes for the aged.

A good air conditioning system should provide constant, year-round control of temperature, humidity, rate of ventilation, and air cleanliness, which can contribute greatly to making the home environment not only healthful, but pleasant. It is therefore important to provide for conversion to total air conditioning in the future, even if the construction budget will not permit such a system initially.

A central air conditioning system is recommended. It should be well engineered and include careful zoning, good filtration of air, and individual private room control of temperature. The system should provide a temperature range of 75–80°F., with relative humidities of 40–50 per cent.

Any of the central duct type systems, or individual room units that are served by central systems, are satisfactory. Self-contained individual room units are not as desirable, and are usually more expensive to maintain. A radiant ceiling heating and cooling system, however, has proved satisfactory.

Well-insulated walls and roof, designed to reduce heat gain and loss, will not only reduce the first cost of the air conditioning system, but will reduce operating costs, thereby amortizing the higher first cost of good construction in a few years.

Elevators

Multistory buildings for homes for the aged have been made possible through the great improvements in automatic elevators. These are now safe and unfrightening, although training in their use will be required for many older people. It should be pointed out that the usual calculations for elevator load (in terms of people per hour) will not apply to the aged. It may be necessary to provide one elevator more than would normally be required, because the residents are slow in boarding and leaving the cars. The total number will, of course, depend on the size of the building.

The elevators must be fully automatic, and doors should be geared so that they close at a very slow speed, about 6 in. per second. Doors should be equipped with an automatic device so that if a person steps between them as they are closing, they will automatically move back to a full open position.

Plant maintenance

The plant maintenance program must be started at the time the building is being designed. The selection of finish materials, equipment, and electrical and mechanical systems must be made with ease of maintenance in mind. The average small home for the aged cannot afford a large maintenance staff able to cope with complex equipment. But inadequate preventive maintenance of such equipment is likely to lead to costly outside repairs.

For this reason it is desirable for the home not only to avoid needlessly complex equipment, but also to hire the most responsible and efficient maintenance engineer it can afford, even though few actual repairs may be attempted. He should be considered one of the key people on the staff.

The extent of a maintenance and repair program to be undertaken by an institution with its own staff should be considered from an economic viewpoint. The cost of providing space, salaries of employees, tools, and repair supplies, must be balanced against the cost of contracting for all maintenance work with local shops. It is common practice for small institutions to contract for regular maintenance service for air conditioning, refrigeration equipment, and elevators, even though they may have a staff for other maintenance and repairs.

The minimum maintenance shop facilities for a small home of approximately 50 residents may consist of a little more than a space of about 200–300 sq. ft. either adjacent to or part of the boiler room. It could be an all-purpose shop containing a workbench and several ventilated and fireproof closets for supplies, paint, and gear. Locked cabinets should be provided for tools.

With such a shop, the engineer, in addition to caring for the boiler room equipment, would be able to make plumbing and electrical repairs and maintain the building generally. Little carpentry and painting would be done by the engineer, and any major work would have to be performed by outside contract.

The extent of repairs undertaken by an institution very often depends on the abilities and resourcefulness of the maintenance staff. It may be an excellent investment to provide a particularly skilled man with all the necessary space, tools, and equipment to repair and paint furniture; to repair plumbing and electrical work; and even to make minor alterations on the premises. Of course, if such work is contemplated, the local building department must be consulted to avoid violating building codes, as these frequently specify that electrical and plumbing work must be done by licensed electricians and plumbers. Safety devices and exhaust ventilation should be provided for power tools.

If the institution is large enough that the anticipated work load justifies a more comprehensive maintenance program, a number of shops may be required—a mechanical shop for plumbing and heating repairs; an electrical shop for repairing and rewiring small parts such as fixtures, lamps, clocks, and the like; and a carpentry shop. If much painting and refinishing is also contemplated, a paint shop should be provided. This shop should preferably be located outside the main building, but in any event should be of fireproof construction and conform to local codes.

The most important piece of equipment required in these shops is a workbench with a heavy plank top, shallow drawers, and ample cabinets below for storage of large and small tools. A machinist's vise and carpenter's vise and a buffer and grinder are usually mounted on this bench. If space permits, a pedestal-mounted buffer and grinder would be more desirable than the bench-mounted type. Also essential are a portable welding outfit and portable pipe vise ready for use in any part of the home for cutting, welding, and threading. A compressed air outlet for blasting dust from work under repair is recommended for each bench.

At the electrician's bench, several duplex receptacles could be installed for 110 and 220 volts in both alternating and direct current, if required, for use in checking different sizes and types of motors under repair. A test board for testing appliances with low voltage is also recommended. A simple board might easily be constructed by the electrician himself. Lighting of a brightness intensity of at least 25 footcandles should be provided at work benches.

Storage cabinets are next in importance. Too much space cannot be provided for the storage of small parts and tools, pipe fittings of all types and sizes, light bulbs, patching material, and the like. Orderly storage and inventory of these numerous items is essential for efficient maintenance. Wall racks are necessary for the proper storage of pipe, tubing, ladders, and scaffolding. Long extension ladders and pipe may be stored in central storage.

Each shop should be provided with a service sink, a stepladder, service truck, and metal locker for each employee. If funds and space permit, a shower for the maintenance department would be desirable.

In the refinishing or paint shop, a glass cutting table and storage racks for glass should be provided. A spray hood with hinged panels at front and sides is desirable. This hood should be fitted with an independent exhaust system to the roof, as should the room itself. The paint storage room should have open metal shelving and exterior wall vents at floor and ceiling. Fireproof partitions with self-closing, metal-covered fire doors and frames should be supplied for the refinishing shop and for paint storage. A small wire-glass view door panel for easy observation in such hazardous shops is recommended.

Ordinary electrical wiring and appliances are generally permitted in shops where painting operations are minor and paint in small quantities is stored in the original closed containers. However, in large institutions where these operations are more extensive, explosion-proof electrical wiring and equipment may be required as specified in the National Board of Fire Underwriters Pamphlet No. 33, "Paint Spraying and Spray Booths." A watchman's check-in station should be located in this vulnerable area to make certain that it is kept under regular surveillance.

9: Construction Materials and Costs

By I. S. Loewenberg, AIA
Loewenberg & Loewenberg, Architects and Engineers, Chicago, Illinois

A home for the aged should be constructed of materials that are easy to maintain and that will not require excessive repairs. It should be able to stand up under the pressure of constant use, and should be so designed that when repairs are necessary, they can be made easily and without disrupting the operation of the home.

The choice of construction methods and finish materials strongly affects both construction and operational budgets. For institutions such as homes for the aged, greater emphasis is normally placed on operational and maintenance considerations than on first construction costs, because operational savings over the life of a building will repay many times over the increased construction costs required to yield these savings. Of course, other advantages are gained through the use of high quality materials and farseeing building techniques.

Construction

The structural frame should be of fire-resistive construction—either skeleton or wallbearing. In selecting an appropriate structural system, it is important that future changes within the building or additions to it be borne in mind. Naturally, the dominant factors should be adaptation to functional layout and economy of means.

The choice of exterior facing materials will depend on the locale and the design, and may include various types of masonry materials, aluminum, porcelain, or steel panels, and so on.

Many new materials and facing systems designed for exterior walls are in use today, and still others are being developed by industry.

The object of many of the building industry's research programs is to find better ways to face buildings. Speed of erection, minimum labor on the site, less space consumption, and better heat insulation all lead to better buildings at lower cost. Exterior panel walls no more than 1½ in. thick, for instance, now made by many manufacturers, are superior in almost every respect to 12-in. masonry walls.

Building insulation against heat loss and heat gain aids comfort and reduces fuel consumption. Every roof needs insulation, if only, as in some parts of the country, to inhibit structural movement of the roof deck and structure. Some roof systems provide both structural strength and insulation in one precast unit. The type of roof system ultimately selected should reflect other structural decisions, such as what floor systems are to be used in multistory buildings. If future vertical expansion is planned, easy removal of roofing and insulation is mandatory.

Flashing and counterflashing, gravel stops, and expansion joints should be copper. To ensure a first-class roof installation, it is advisable to obtain a 15- or 20-year bond. The slight additional cost is justified by the results.

Windows may be constructed of wood, steel, bronze, aluminum, or stainless steel. They may be double-hung, casement, projected, sliding, or simply hinged ventilators. The windows of multistory buildings must be capable of being washed from inside the building or from a movable, suspended platform.

Doors may be flush wood veneer or steel. Door frames should be hollow metal except when special design considerations exist. Generally, all doors more than 3 ft. wide should have three hinges. Door holders on resident room doors are useful to prevent slamming. Door closers and panic hardware should be provided as required by codes and administrative practice. All locks should be master keyed.

Partitions should be of fire-resistive construction. Cinder block, gypsum block, hollow clay tile, and solid plaster on metal lath or steel partitions may all be used. Partitions, generally, should provide sound reduction at least equal to that of 4-in. cinder block plastered both sides.

Wall and floor finishes

Wall finishes in a home for the aged should be selected for long-term wearability and ease of maintenance. At the same time the finishes should not be so completely utilitarian that the home will have an institutional character. Still another factor is the need to stretch the construction dollar as far as possible.

The designer must keep in mind that walls and floors of homes for the aged have special requirements. Carts used to distribute supplies can mar walls and floors. Older people are likely to touch corridor walls for support at times, even though handrails may be present. The floors must provide a sure footing for the residents.

Ceilings in corridors, dining rooms, kitchens, utility rooms, bathrooms, residence rooms, offices, and miscellaneous rooms used by the residents should have acoustic ceilings. The principle of arresting noise at its source might well imply that all ceilings should act, at least to some extent, as sound barriers.

In areas such as lounges, recreation rooms, lobbies, and the like, finishes that require little maintenance can still provide color, warmth, and interest.

For most of the areas used by the residents, including the infirmary, a hard plaster finish for walls is ordinarily adequate. A high quality paint should be applied to it according to manufacturers' specifications. Such a finish would require repainting every three or four years, depending on the kind of care given the walls.

For a more durable wall finish, consideration should be given to the various sheet plastics. They may be wainscot or ceiling high. They will usually not show hand marks or be marred by carts, and need never be refinished. Sheet plastics, particularly desirable in corridors, dining rooms, and recreation areas, come in a variety of colors and patterns. Their occasionally higher first cost is offset by their lower maintenance requirements over the years.

Ceramic wall tile, of course, is the preferred finish for bath rooms, toilets, and utility rooms. Ceramic mosaic tile should be used on the floor in these locations, and may be installed around or behind lavatories in residence rooms.

Floor materials that are quiet, durable, and resilient, such as linoleum and rubber, asphalt, or vinyl tile are preferable throughout except in kitchens, bathrooms, toilet rooms, janitor's closets and service areas.

Asphalt tile is probably the most economical floor finish. It is easily installed, comes in many colors, is durable, and will give long service if properly maintained. It does have a disadvantage, however, in that it will dent badly if heavy furniture or equipment rests on it and is expensive to maintain.

Vinyl tile is more durable, more easily maintained, and does not dent so easily as asphalt tile, but it is more expensive. Rubber tile is also expensive, but provides greater comfort underfoot than either asphalt or vinyl. The pamphlet, *Characteristics of Resilient Floor Materials Commonly Used in Hospitals*, distributed by the U.S. Public Health Service, is useful in choosing among these floors.

Cork tile makes for a very handsome and comfortable floor. It could be used to advantage in lounges and resident areas where there is no cart traffic and where a more expensive floor finish is warranted. Because of the difficulties they may cause to users of wheelchairs and crutches, carpeting and rugs are not recommended as a desirable floor covering except in special areas, and then they should be firmly secured at the edges.

The service area finishes must, of course, be durable and, particularly in the kitchen, easily cleaned. Glazed structural units might be used in these areas. These are structural tiles having one surface glazed with the color fired in, and are suitable for corridors, stair halls, and other parts of the service areas. The large joints necessary for some of this material make its use for the kitchen somewhat questionable, although it is often used there. Applied ceramic wall tile could be more easily cleaned, as the joints are usually much narrower. Hard plaster and paint would require frequent maintenance in these areas, and while the first cost of this finish is less than that of glazed structural units, it would probably be more expensive in the long run.

A smooth surface should always be provided for the kitchen ceiling. Perforated types of acoustical ceilings should be avoided, as they can become a very difficult maintenance problem. Plastic-surfaced acoustic tile form a satisfactory ceiling.

The shops and storage areas require only that structural walls be finished with smooth joints and covered with a masonry paint.

The floors of the service areas, except for the kitchen, may be smooth concrete. The surface of the concrete should be treated with a hardener to eliminate dusting.

The best material for kitchens has proved to be quarry tile floor and base, with tile wainscoting. With special joint material, quarry tile is greaseproof. Its slip resistance is generally satisfactory, but for special areas (around ranges, for example) tiles with an abrasive aggregate can

be used. It would be a mistake to choose a substitute material because of a lower first cost alone.

Fire safety

Because residents of a home for the aged may be active and yet suffer from physical and mental infirmities, it is most important that the basic principles of fire safety be followed in the design of such homes.

The proper selection of materials and equipment can reduce the chance of a fire starting in the first place, and help localize it once started. A home for the aged must be of fire-resistive construction even though some codes may permit otherwise.

If building codes exist, they ordinarily describe the requirements for this type of construction. However, if local codes are not complete and up-to-date, or do not exist, the recommendations of established national organizations dealing with construction and safety, such as the National Board of Fire Underwriters, Underwriters Laboratories, Inc., the National Bureau of Standards, and the like, must be followed.

All buildings housing the aged should be equipped with automatic fire detection and alarm systems. Some of the systems in use today are actuated by heat and some by smoke. An internal signaling system should be installed to sound an alarm at strategic locations in the building, primarily to notify the staff. A manually operated fire alarm should also be provided, preferably connected to a nearby fire station. Every home for the aged should also be equipped with a proper number and kind of portable fire extinguishers. Standpipes within the building and fire hydrants outside are required for the use of the fire department.

If a building or any part of it is of nonfireproof construction, the part so constructed should have sprinklers throughout. No new structure should be built without at least a one-hour fire rating throughout, and a first rate fire alarm system.

The Public Health Service regulations on sprinkler systems are as follows:

"To reduce the danger from fire, it is desirable to provide automatic sprinkler systems in those areas that are considered hazardous from a fire safety point of view. Such hazardous areas may include the soiled linen rooms, basement corridors, paint shops, woodworking shops, trash rooms, storage rooms, accessible attics, laundry and trash chutes, and entire nonfireproofed buildings."

The home should have enough (and large enough) exits for rapid evacuation if necessary. Dead-end corridors should be avoided, and in multistory buildings the stairways should be located so that no pockets are formed in which residents may be trapped. Stairways should be fully enclosed, and all stair exit doors should be fire doors bearing the Underwriters Laboratories seal of approval.

Doors leading to stairways should be the swinging type, and should open in the direction of exit travel without blocking the stairway or the operation of other doors. All exit doors should have illuminated signs. Exterior doors should swing outward.

Building costs

Cost is probably the most important factor in institutional work, for the basic reason that the organization planning the work must determine what costs will be incurred and then obtain the funds necessary to complete the building program. The architect is called upon for a reasonable estimate of the costs so that the building committee of any institution may know where it stands.

Fortunately, reasonable estimates can be made by experienced cost estimators, but there are many traps for the inexperienced. The most common of the incorrect methods of estimating is the so-called "per bed" system, in which the number of beds is multiplied by an arbitrary amount to determine the total cost of the project. The fallacy of this method lies in the fact that a home for the aged maintains services that do not vary directly with size. For instance, the service facilities would be more or less the same for a home with 50 beds as for one with 25. The kitchen for a 50-bed home would not have to be twice as large as that for a 25-bed home, nor would the occupational or physical therapy departments, or the medical, administrative, or staff facilities.

A second method of estimating that gives rise to errors when used by the unwary is the determination of cost based on a given floor area per bed. This system is unsatisfactory for the same reasons as those given in the preceding paragraph. Also, many institutions must be designed to provide for future expansion, so that facilities other than the number of beds must be scaled with this need in mind.

To achieve the accurate cost estimates that are so necessary in institutional work, the architect must work closely with the building committee in the development of the project, from its inception to the start of construction.

First, the building committee and the architect should meet to determine a preliminary program, which defines the scope of the services to be provided and the number of residents that will be cared for. The program should be based on an accurate survey of the needs of the community and the ability of the community to support the institution. At these preliminary planning sessions, the pros and cons of the program of care can be discussed until an understanding is reached. Some of the questions to be considered are: type and extent of facilities, equipment, construction materials, site, adaptability of site, and so on.

From this information, rough sketches and basic specifications can be prepared, and a preliminary estimate may be drawn up either by the architect or by an experienced contractor.

This estimate should include the complete costs of the building and site, including equipment, mechanical facilities, and furnishings. When these rough schematic drawings have been approved, work can start on a more detailed set. As the drawings become more accurate, a more reliable cost figure can be given.

Checking before the plans are complete may indicate whether costs are too high, and if necessary, provisions can be made to lower them before sending the plans out for final bids. If adequate cost controls are maintained throughout the planning stages, the actual cost of the institution should be reasonably close to the estimates.

The major units of cost involved in the construction of a home for the aged are:

1. *Plant*   Building, site, site improvements, and contingencies for anticipated changes

2. *Equipment*   Furniture, kitchenware and linen, and the like

3. *Preparation*   Site survey, soil investigation, architect's fee, supervision and inspection at site, legal fees, and cost of fund raising.

Geographic location has a strong influence on building costs. Regional factors include climate, building codes, labor costs, transportation, and the like. Generally, building costs tend to be higher in the larger cities, where there are strong unions, rigid building codes, and competition for the available labor force. Costs are usually lower away from the influence of the large city. However, lower labor costs may reflect lower productivity, so that it is important to be familiar with all the characteristics of an area before making a cost estimate.

Timing is an important factor in taking bids. Bids taken during periods of low building activity may be lower than when contractors are busy and generally overextended.

It should also be recognized that a cost estimate given at any particular time may vary considerably a few years later. Costs of labor and materials have been rising constantly during the past decade, and this condition will probably persist as long as our economy continues to expand.

(For some examples of actual costs, please see Appendix B.)

10: Design

By Edward H. Noakes
Edward H. Noakes & Associates, Architects, Bethesda, Maryland

From the standpoint of architectural experience, the aged have remained a neglected and even mysterious segment of society. With few exceptions, sheltered care for the aged has been provided in old buildings that became available because they outlived the purposes for which they were originally built. As a consequence, there is no continuing thread of development from which the architect involved in this field for the first time can take instruction.

The new prospect for our later years that is being rapidly developed by medicine and the social sciences—a dynamic philosophy of living in old age—requires a totally new physical framework. To architecture, housing for this period of life is a new building type, whose present vague outline will be clarified as more examples are built, and as experience is gained and widely exchanged.

Now, at the beginning of this evolutionary process, the problem may be stated in general terms. Solutions to parts of the problem may be sought in other building types. Thus we look to hospitals for nursing care planning, to apartments and private dwellings for residential living, and to hotels and community centers for group activities. Research in these and other related fields is rewarding, but only to the extent that it forms a more or less technical basis from which we can go on to the central task of understanding and designing for the realities and subtleties of old age.

For instance, compared to an architect's usual clients the aged possess fewer physical and mental resources, and their flexibility and adaptability is markedly reduced. Their sensitivity to extremes of temperature, light, and noise is increased. They are no longer robust. As little of their energy as possible should be expended in adapting either physically or emotionally to their environment.

Careful attention to even minor details can often make the difference between a pleasant and a frustrating existence. Thought and study given to bedroom and bathroom doors and hardware can make life in a wheelchair or on crutches tolerable, rather than an unending series of annoyances. Adequate doorway and corridor dimensions can allow a bed-ridden person to attend communal activities and spend time with companions in the lounge. Proper design of thresholds, steps, windowsill heights and the like can prevent them from becoming major barriers to movement and view. Thus what appears to be a slight inconvenience to a younger person may well be a serious problem to an older one.

No less important than these considerations are the less tangible aspects of a building—those aspects that may raise mere functional competence to the status of architecture. The way things look is important to everyone in varying degrees, depending upon the individual. This same variation in the individual's ability to appreciate beauty exists, of course, among the aged as well, but with special emphasis. The long years of relative inactivity in a home give them the time, probably lacking

63

before, for contemplation and detailed observation.

A well-designed home is a source of pride and affection. A building designed by a mediocre or flashy talent rapidly becomes a source of boredom, if not ridicule. Without beauty, a home for the aged can be no more than an institution for sheltered care; it certainly cannot be a home. In an endless number of ways, thoughtful and skilled designing can provide a rich variety of vistas, textures, colors, and materials, in recognition of the great range in tastes and needs of older persons and their accentuated individuality.

Through design, the architect can provide symbols of protection and security for the residents as they move about the home. Some residents will relish the challenge of floor-to-ceiling glass opening directly on the street. Others may require the primitive feeling of safety symbolized by a fireplace in a cave. Outside and inside may be welded in a certain area, and elsewhere may be solidly separated.

We can use the familiar natural textures and colors of wood, stone, and brick and contrast them with more sophisticated materials like glass or painted plaster. We can use planting areas indoors and out; both bold and quiet draperies and upholstery; ceiling textures and colors that define areas; different ceiling heights; varying patterns and kinds of ceiling lighting fixtures; views outside into intimate courts and views into the far distance; colors that are occasionally brilliant in limited areas for accents; sculpture inside and out; fireplaces inside and out for barbecues; hung paintings and painted or mosaic murals; and so on. Pervading everything should be a sense of order and security, of warmth and use that denote a home, and of scale and proportion that represent an individual rather than a group.

Architecture, being both an art and a technology, must span the range from the purely esthetic to the purely practical. As the architect develops his designs, appropriate weight must be given both aspects of his task if he is to help in making added years richer ones. His art must be guided by a sympathetic understanding of the emotional and mental state of the aged, just as his technology is shaped by knowledge of the special limitations imposed by the frailties of their bodies.

11: The Function of the Architect

By Edwin B. Morris, Jr., AIA
Assistant to the Director, American Institute of Architects

In keeping with our rapidly developing society, the architectural profession has expanded enormously in complexity and quality of services. One hundred years ago the architect was concerned principally with the problem of providing shelter for a pioneer society that was expanding its boundaries and bridging its frontiers. Today the architect must consider man's physical environment in relation to all of the following: new social aspirations; physical infirmities; economic status; spiritual needs; a host of new contrivances; and new problems of population shifts, land use, and urban congestion.

The architect's training equips him to design and supervise the construction of buildings and facilities tailored to the special desires and particular needs of his client. In the special field of homes for the aged, which is new and growing fast, the administrators or trustees often know what must be done for the resident and what they plan to do for him, but have no way of translating these needs and plans into physical spaces and functional relationships.

The architect assumes the responsibility for the planning and construction of a building that must be economical, efficient, practical, and pleasant to look at—and that will last, for better or worse, for generations. In performing this task he must direct an immensely varied team of highly qualified specialists.

At the same time, from the day he is engaged until the end of a building operation, and even thereafter, the architect is the client's professional adviser and representative. He must assist in drawing contracts, adhering to building codes and other regulations, preparing contract documents, letting contracts, certifying construction changes, and seeing throughout that the owner gets what he pays for.

The architect is the one person on the whole building scene who can serve the client's interest objectively, because he is under no compulsion from manufacturers or contractors. He is the only person who can appraise the merits of any aspect of the over-all project impartially—before its design is undertaken and during the subsequent process of design and construction.

This matter of personal representation and protection of the owner's interest is of prime importance, and raises the question of how the liaison between the client and the architect can be best handled. Often the board of trustees of the home for the aged is the client. Usually, this board delegates its authority to a building committee which, through its chairman, selects the architect and deals directly with him throughout the course of the project.

The building committee should be carefully selected to ensure that it represents the financial, administrative, and operative knowledge and interests of the home and its board. This arrangement (of having only one responsible person or group dealing directly with the architect) can provide a smooth working arrangement and eliminate the many misunderstandings that can arise when many people are at liberty to approach the architect with their individual problems, requirements, and often inexperienced "solutions."

In this most complicated of all processes—building a building—the architect's function is to assume the client's responsibilities and to solve the inherent complexities. It is the client's job to select the architect and to work with him until the completion of the project.

Architect selection

The architect should be engaged as soon as a building is contemplated. The administrator, building committee, and medical and nursing staffs should sit down with the architect at the very start, and all physical needs should be incorporated into a written planning program before a single line is drawn. This program then becomes the basis for the physical layout, and the home authorities can be assured that their needs will be met without misunderstandings or questions on basic matters during the progress of the job.

Two methods of selecting the architect are generally used. The first method is direct selection, or selection through personal knowledge or on the basis of reputation, demonstrated ability, and the recommendations of others for whom the architect has rendered service.

The second method is comparative selection, or selection from a group of architects who are given an opportunity to present evidence of their qualifications before the building committee. Quite naturally, there would be a number of questions to be asked of architects who presented their qualifications on a comparative basis. It would be advisable for the building committee to consult with an architect on how these interviews might be set up. The local chapter of the American Institute of Architects might be helpful in answering such questions.

Architect's services

After the architect has been selected, there are a number of ways in which the client can help, both immediately and as the project pro-

gresses. The architect is the professional adviser and agent of the client. This relationship requires mutual trust and confidence. The client should clearly outline his building needs and frankly state the amount of money that can be spent. The architect may then help in budgeting all costs involved, not only for construction, but for equipment, furnishings, site improvements, and landscaping as well. In this way it can be determined at the outset whether building needs and funds are compatible.

The client should have the architect advise him on the selection of a site, particularly on its size, suitability, topography, and the availability of utilities. When the site is selected, the client obtains or authorizes the architect to obtain all information on boundaries, contours, trees, pavements, adjoining properties, rights-of-way, restrictions, easements, locations of utilities, plans of existing buildings to be altered, if any, and the like. If any unusal sub-surface conditions such as rock or unstable earth are suspected, the client furnishes test borings or pits.

The client should make sure that he completely understands the plans as the architect develops them, so that costly delays and changes will not occur later.

Normal architectural services are usually rendered in sequence in three stages: preliminary; working drawings and specifications; and construction.

The preliminary stage generally includes the following:

1. Conferences to determine the scope of the project—purposes, general plan and design, feasibility, general type of construction, mechanical equipment, probable time required to build, and approximate cost and means of financing.

2. Visits to the site by the architect to study the project placement.

3. Examination of laws, ordinances, codes, standards, rules and regulations of controlling

agencies, and study of the requirements of insurance carriers.

4. Preparation of schematic studies of the building and its relation to the site. These are discussed at each stage with the client. The architect amplifies the schematic studies with recommendations on type of construction, materials, and mechanical equipment, and states the probable cost and construction time required.

5. Preparation of comprehensive preliminary drawings and outline specifications in sufficient detail to define the final scope of the project and to make possible a realistic cost estimate.

Upon acceptance by the client of the preliminary documents described above, the first stage of services is completed. This acceptance by the client is an implicit agreement that changes will not be made throughout the rest of the project. The reason that so much emphasis is placed on the preliminary stage is that changes may be made with little trouble or cost at this point, whereas they become very costly and time-consuming during subsequent stages of the building process.

The working drawings and specifications and related documents represent what the building will be like in every detail when it is finished. In this stage the architect:

1. Develops the preliminary drawings into working drawings to include all technical information needed for accurate bidding and final construction.

2. Includes all essential architectural, structural, plumbing, heating, electrical, and other mechanical and site improvement drawings.

3. Coordinates drawings and specifications for all trades to avoid conflicts and to facilitate proper installations.

4. Prepares technical specifications describing the type and quality of materials and equipment, their finish, and the manner and places in which they are used by each trade.

6. Assists in obtaining approval of controlling government agencies when required.

7. Furnishes the necessary or agreed number of sets of drawings and specifications for bidding and construction.

Upon completion of working drawings and specifications the second stage of services is completed. At this time it is possible for the client to know exactly what his building will be like, both functionally and esthetically. During this second stage the architect also keeps a running appraisal of estimated costs. If at any time it appears that costs may rise above the preliminary estimates, it is his obligation to inform his client, so that necessary adjustments can be made.

In *the construction stage* the architect assists with proposals and contracts and supervises construction. Generally speaking, he:

1. Advises on the qualifications of prospective bidders.

2. Assists in preparing proposal forms and construction contract forms, and manages advertising for bids, the receiving and opening of bids, and the awarding of contracts.

3. Gives all instructions to the contractor. It is important that the client issue all his instructions through the architect.

4. Checks shop drawings and samples submitted by the contractor and prepares any supplemental drawings or large-scale details needed to clarify the contract drawings.

5. Makes periodic inspection of the construction at intervals (normally averaging one a week) deemed necessary by him to ascertain whether the work is being executed in conformity with contract requirements, and suggests full-time supervision at additional cost to the client when the character of the project so warrants.

6. Directs and evaluates all required tests of materials.

7. Advises the client on progress and quality of construction.

8. Prepares, checks costs of, and issues change orders covering modifications of the contract.

9. Checks the contractors' applications for payments, and issues certificates authorizing such payments.

10. Sees to it that the required written guarantees are delivered to the client.

11. When satisfied that all terms of construction contracts have been fulfilled, accepts the completed project on behalf of the client and issues certification to that effect to the client and contractor and, when required, to surety and insurance carriers.

Upon certification by the architect that all contracts under his supervision have been fulfilled, the architect's normal services are completed. It is proper for the client to retain reproduced sets of drawings and specifications for use in servicing and maintaining the building. However, all drawings and specifications are instruments of service and the property of the architect, and may not be used on other work except by agreement with the architect.

Quite naturally, the question of cost of architectural services will arise. This cost is not insignificant and should not be, because a good workman is worthy of his hire. For his responsibility for the complex planning procedures and his direction of the team that accomplishes them, the architect is generally paid a fee based on a percentage of the final cost of the building.

All the services listed above are provided for by this fee, and with it the architect must pay his engineers or other consultants, his payroll and other overhead, and of course, obtain his own profit. In addition to the services normally included, other services may sometimes be required, and the additional charges incurred for them should be agreed upon before they are rendered. Examples of such services are:

1. Preparation of special display drawings, models, or perspectives.

2. Full-time supervision or services of a resident supervisor (clerk of the works).

3. Reproduction of drawings and specifications beyond the number stated in the architect's agreement.

4. Major changes requested by the client after preliminary drawings are approved or after detailed work is completed on the working drawings.

5. Administering construction work let on a "cost-plus" basis.

6. Designing furniture, fixtures, and decorative work, or assisting in the selection or purchase of such items.

7. Serving as an expert witness.

8. Consultations, when no other architectural services are required.

9. Special travel in the interest of the client.

10. Detailed construction cost estimates.

11. Measured drawings of existing buildings to be altered.

12. Extra supervision resulting from unduly protracted construction periods through causes beyond the architect's control.

13. As-built drawings when required.

As a general rule, the architect saves the owner a sum much larger than his fee in the actual cost of construction. His contribution enhances the value of the finished job even more because he designs for savings in maintenance and operating costs. Carefully weighed against the total costs of construction, operation, and maintenance, the architect's fee on a project is one of the best construction bargains available.

The American Institute of Architects nationally and through its 126 chapters throughout the country stands ready to render as much help as possible to building committees and others interested in building. Through its research facilities and liaison with other groups in the construction industry—contractors, engineers, financing agencies and many others—the AIA has become the source of almost every form and document necessary to the operation of the construction industry.

The architect who enters this new field is faced with a tremendous challenge and a public obligation. An immense amount of research, hard work, common sense, and good thinking must be applied to the job.

The home for the aged presents an unparalleled opportunity for architects to do something for the public good, to enhance their own professional stature, and to elevate the architectural profession. But even more important is the contribution they can make to the health, welfare, and happiness of older people.

SECTION II: PRIZE WINNING DESIGNS

*An architectural competition for the design
of a home for the aged, held in 1956*

Advisory Committee

Michael M. Dacso, M.D., Director
Physical Medicine & Rehabilitation
Goldwater Memorial Hospital

John J. Egan, President
Hospital Industries Association

Emerson Goble, Managing Editor
Architectural Record

Frank S. Groner, Administrator
Baptist Memorial Hospital

Everett W. Jones, Vice President
The Modern Hospital Publishing Co.

I. S. Loewenberg
Loewenberg & Loewenberg
Architects and Engineers

Edward H. Noakes
White, Noakes & Neubauer
Architects and Engineers

Ollie A. Randall, Vice Chairman
National Committee on the Aging

Dean W. Roberts, M.D., Director
Commission on Chronic Illness

August Hoenack, Chief
Architectural & Engineering Division of
    Hospital & Medical Facilities
    U. S. Public Health Service

Walter A. Taylor, Director
Department of Education & Research
American Institute of Architects

Wilbur Henry Tusler
Magney, Tusler & Setter
Architects and Engineers
Chairman of the Committee on
    Hospitalization and Public Health
    of the American Institute of Architects

Joseph Douglas Weiss
Architect

Clifford Wolfe, Secretary
Council on Hospital Planning and
    Plant Operation
American Hospital Association

Committee Secretary:
    Geneva Mathiasen,
    National Committee on the Aging

CONDITIONS OF THE COMPETITION

Approval

The Program and method of procedure have been approved by the Committee on Architectural Competitions of the American Institute of Architects.

Eligibility

This competition is open to all architects, architectural students and draftsmen except those regularly employed by the professional adviser, the consulting architect or any of the judges. Presentation may be made by individuals or collaborative groups.

Professional Adviser

The sponsor has retained as its Professional Adviser, I. S. Loewenberg, A.I.A. All correspondence should be addressed as follows:

> Professional Adviser
> Home for the Aged Competition
> Suite 517
> 1145 19th Street, N. W.
> Washington 6, D. C.

Consulting Architect

> Edward H. Noakes

Awards

The following awards will be made for the winning presentations selected by the Jury of Awards:

First Prize	$5,000.00
Second Prize	$2,500.00
Third Prize	$1,000.00
Three Honorable Mentions (each)	$ 500.00

Jury of Awards

Chairman:

Pietro Belluschi, F.A.I.A., Dean,
School of Architecture and Planning
Massachusetts Institute of Technology

William Wilson Wurster, F.A.I.A., Dean
School of Architecture
University of California

Richard J. Adams, A.I.A.
Sherlock, Smith and Adams
Architects and Engineers
Montgomery, Alabama

Ollie A. Randall
Vice Chairman
National Committee on the Aging

Charles F. Wilinsky, M.D.
Hospital Consultant
Boston, Massachusetts

THE PROBLEM

I. **Site**

The contestant is free to select his own site. It may be in an urban or suburban area, in a small or large community anywhere in the continental United States or Canada. It is suggested that wherever possible, site selection should be based on a real piece of property selected by the contestant as best suited for a Home for the Aged.

II. **Capacity**

The home shall provide for a total of 100 residents of which 75 shall be housed in resident units and 25 in an infirmary. The direction of expansion of both resident units and infirmary shall be indicated on the plot plan.

III. **Administration**

Entrance lobby with adjacent public toilets and telephone booths. Both toilets and telephone booths to be capable of use by residents in wheelchairs.

Private offices for the administrator with adjacent living room and toilet; social services director; and nursing service director.

General office for 3 secretaries or typists with clothes closet and storage.

Telephone switchboard and information desk adjacent to general office and close to but not obtrusively controlling the main entrance.

Conference room with coat closet. Also available for resident use.

IV. **Central Facilities**

1. Living —

    Main lounge to seat 30 in informal conversation groups.
    Two small living rooms near main entrance for private entertainment of visitors by residents.

2. Dining —

    Main dining room close to main lounge to seat 100 at 4 and 6 seat tables.

3. Recreation —

    Multi-purpose room to seat 100 for movies, lectures, dances and community activities shall be capable of division into smaller areas. Provide a projector booth and chair storage.

4. Shop —

    Facility for sale of gifts, articles made by residents, cigarettes, magazines, coffee and sandwiches.

5. Religion —

    Chapel may be small area for 8 or 10 persons with folding wall towards multi-purpose room for major attendance at services.

6. Library —

    Space for quiet reading and study for 6 or 8 persons. Provide about 100 linear feet of book shelves with counter, sink and storage for small book truck.

V. Resident Units

To promote a residential scale, it is suggested that no more than 30 residents be grouped in one unit. In each unit about 90% of the residents should have private rooms with the remainder in double rooms.

1. Resident's rooms shall be planned to permit at least two furniture arrrangements, one of them with the head against the wall and 3 feet wide access space on either side to permit ease of bed care when required. Rooms at grade may have access to the outside. Each room shall have a water closet and lavatory in a private toilet. At least 10% of the private toilets shall be planned for use by residents in wheelchairs. Each room to possess a general clothes closet and space for an easy chair, a desk with a chair, and a chest of drawers as a minimum. Minimum room area, including closets, is 125 sq. ft. for a single room and 200 sq. ft. for a double room. A space shall be provided for storage of a collapsible wheelchair readily available from the patient's bed.

2. The living area in each unit shall include a living room to seat 60% of the residents in arm chairs and couches. A small kitchen alcove shall be adjacent. Provide a telephone booth large enough for wheelchair residents. Provisions shall be made for the use of a central TV set with minimum interference with other residents. One or more spaces to seat no more than 5 persons shall be located away from the living room. Access to outside (porches, terraces, etc.) is desirable.

3. Bathing facilities in each unit shall be centrally located and arranged for visual privacy and ease of supervision. Bath tubs shall be provided on the basis of one for 10 residents, and showers on the basis of one for 10 residents. Bath tubs to have three side access. There shall be a separate bathroom for each sex. For the purposes of this competition, the ratio in each unit will be about 4 men to 6 women. There shall be a toilet adjacent to each bathroom, planned for use by residents in wheelchairs.

4. Space in each unit shall be provided for linen storage, janitors closet and staff toilet.

5. Each unit shall have a nurses station with charting space, and medicine preparation and storage space. A utility room with work space and bed-pan washing facilities shall be provided adjacent. These facilities should be minimum and planned to be unobtrusive and secure when not in use.

VI. Infirmary

Bed distribution should be approximately 5 beds in private rooms, 12 beds in double rooms and 8 beds in 4 bed rooms.

1. Residents' rooms shall be planned for nursing ease, for visual privacy in the 2 and 4 bed rooms when needed and every resident should have as unrestricted a view outside as possible. Each room shall have a private toilet with water closet and lavatory planned for use by wheelchair patients. Clothes lockers or closets are required for each resident. A space shall be provided for storage of a collapsible wheelchair readily available to the resident's bed.

2. A nurses station with charting and medicine storage and preparation space shall be centrally located. A utility room with clean and soiled space shall be adjacent. A nurses' toilet shall be nearby. An examining and treatment room shall be provided. Consideration should be given to the prompt disposal of soiled linen.

3. Bathing facilities for unit shall consist of a bathroom with one tub and three-side access and one shower arranged for visual privacy but ease of supervision. A toilet shall be immediately adjacent to the bathroom and also accessible from the main corridor, planned to serve also as a training toilet for the wheelchair patients. There shall be a bathroom for each sex.

4. A combined lounge and dining area shall be provided with a minimum area based on 50 sq. ft. per bed for 75% of infirmary beds. The dining area should seat 75% of the total infirmary accommodations. The lounge area, separated by a movable partition should comfortably seat the same number. A small snack kitchen shall be provided.

5. A linen closet, janitor's closet and wheelchair and stretcher storage shall be provided.

6. Store room for equipment (oxygen tents, dressing carts, etc.)

Note: In planning the infirmary, consideration should be given to the delivery of meals from the kitchen. It is also important to consider the speedy and private removal of those who have died.

VII. **Health Maintenance Facilities**

The following shall be provided:

1. Doctors office with adjacent examining room.
2. Laboratory for routine blood and urine analysis.
3. EKG and BMR room adjacent to laboratory.
4. Dental room with one chair.
5. Eye, ear, nose and throat examining and treatment room.
6. Physical medicine suite shall include:
   Office for therapist (glass enclosed).
   Occupational therapy work shop.
   Exercise room.
   2 Electro-Therapy booths.
   1 hydro-therapy booth.
   Storage for linen and portable equipment.
7. Radiographic suite shall include:
   Radiography and fluoroscopy room with control booth.
   Dark room.
8. Barber and Beauty shop with a booth for a Podiatrist.
9. Waiting space for all facilities bearing in mind a number of wheelchair residents.
10. Doctor's lounge and locker room with toilet.
11. Staff and patient toilets.
12. Ambulance (and undertaker's) entrance.

VIII. **Service Facilities**

The following shall be provided:

1. Service entrance.
2. Main kitchen —
   Receiving, storage, preparation of special diets, serving and dishwashing.
   Dieticians office.
   Garbage storage and can washing.

3. Staff —
    Dining room to seat 16 at 4 seat tables.
    Staff lounge adjacent to dining room.

4. Stores —
    Receiving, storage and dispatching of general supplies. (10 sq. ft. per resident)
    Storage of oxygen tanks.
    Store room for resident's belongings. (15 sq. ft. per resident minimum)

5. Maintenance —
    Shop for carpentry, electrical, plumbing and painting with material storage.
    Space for grounds maintenance equipment.

6. Mechanical —
    Boiler room.

7. Lockers —
    Nurses locker room for 6 with lounge and toilets.
    Female help locker room for 15 with lounge and toilets.
    Male help locker room for 8 with toilets.

8. **Laundry room for residents use provided with 2 washers, 2 dryers and 2 ironing boards.**

9. **Garage for 3 cars.**

COMMENTS BY THE CHAIRMAN OF THE JURY

By Pietro Belluschi, FAIA, Dean of the School of Architecture and Planning, Massachusetts Institute of Technology

This competition was motivated by the desire to find likely solutions to the problem of housing our older people. While the results were judged by the usual architectural standards, they must also be viewed in a much larger social context.

Architects, particularly the younger ones, take pride in the fact that they are becoming more aware of human and social values. They believe that if their profession has made contributions of any great value to our present civilization, it has not been in erecting monuments or palaces or cathedrals or grand-scale city plans, but in creating establishments for the use and comfort of the average human being.

The rapid industrial growth of the last century had tended to fragment and isolate the individual. Slums and dark factories were the products of our early industrialization. Human beings, with few exceptions, were treated as cogs in a vast machine, to be used and expended; illness, misery, and the needs of old age were of little or no concern to society.

In this nightmare, the architect was seldom called upon to plan; he was in fact little more than an elegant decorator in the service of the very rich, mostly to satisfy their desire to create the symbols of their wealth and power. Thus the training of an architect was based mainly on a superficial knowledge of the plush and pompous externals of the dead past. Only in the last few decades has architecture been asked to give order and form to the new concepts growing out of a responsible and humane society.

Modern architects have been accused, of course, and perhaps with some justification, of not knowing how to design monumental buildings; but you will see them using their skill and imagination in giving a warmly human touch to hospitals, kindergartens, schools, factories, housing projects, recreation centers, and churches. We may say that the real evolution in architecture is not, as many people think, merely an abandonment of cornices and Greek columns and fancy pediments mistakenly labeled "classic design," but the acceptance of a deeper and more difficult task, that of giving order and form and meaning to a society that believes in using its great wealth for the benefit of every citizen, wealthy or poor. That much has yet to be done is apparent to everyone.

The vast growth of our population, the need to renew the old and obsolete portions of almost every American city, the great increase in our material wealth, the lengthening of our life span—all these factors are already imposing problems of a magnitude unknown to previous generations.

This competition for a home for the aged is

very much a part of the picture I have described, and the solutions entered by many architects confirmed the maturity of approach taken by our profession, particularly by the younger members. The competition, if nothing else, has given us a glimpse of the many ways in which the problem can be met, and perhaps even more has shown the necessity of defining its limits.

The architects who will be asked to design these homes in the future must be told clearly for whom they are to build, that is, how old are the persons to be housed, what kind of care they should receive, how much freedom they should have. Someone must decide how much our society can afford to do. Should we attempt to make it so easy and attractive for men and women of minimum social security age (I mean 62–65 years old) to live in such ideal conditions that all our resources will be exhausted before we can take care of the older people and more helpless cases? Should we think of residents of homes for the aged as people beginning a new and more sheltered life, where all the opportunities of social contact are preserved and even enhanced, or are we to give more weight to the ones who need protective and health care?

These are not idle questions; they have their advocates and their merits, but all of them will directly and indirectly affect the selection of site, the expenditures of funds, the size of the establishment, and above all the design of the plans and details of the buildings that are to shelter the aged.

The jury was conscious of the complexity of the problem but endeavored to judge each entry on the bases that were wisely outlined in the program, that is: plan relationship, which means a clear, simple, and practical plan; economy of space, which of course means not only first-cost economy but also economy in administration; quality of environment, which means architectural merit, if this is understood to mean a sensitive use of space and a concern for the appropriateness of scale, color, light, and for the graciousness of detailing; and finally,

structural practicability, which is also a test of good over-all design and of economy of means.

The winning design by J. J. Jordan and Hanford Yang of Philadelphia was the unanimous choice of the committee. It seems to combine in a rare and self-assured manner the best qualities of all other entries. The plan has logic and clarity; it suggests space pleasant to live in and easy to supervise and administer. The clinical facilities, although separate, are convenient and well located in relation to the administrative unit. The recreation area is in a most appropriate relationship to the living units; these in turn have been so designed as to create a gracious environment.

The exterior design is restrained yet warm, and appropriate without affectation, depending on good relationship of space and on the garden-like courts to obtain a homelike effect, rather than on superficial or fashionable tricks. The jury was very happy to recommend it as an excellent example to be studied with care, although not necessarily to be adopted without taking into consideration the special conditions that will always affect individual projects.

The project that placed second, entered by Alfred and Jane West Clauss of the firm of Bellante & Clauss, was thought by the jury to possess many of the virtues of the first award, although its plan has less clarity, and the circulation is not as good. The layout of the infirmary is very efficient, perhaps more so than that of the first-prize winner, yet it is not so accessible to administration or services, even if a case can be made for placing it on the second floor. Of the two or three similar schemes having clustered living units, this was not the most brilliant from an esthetic point of view, but was the most easily defended in terms of circulation and relationship of the units to the intervening courts.

The exterior design was good even if a little self-conscious in the treatment of roofs; all in all, the jury felt it possessed great qualities of warmth and a pleasant human scale.

The third-prize winner, by Gerhardt Liebmann of New York, won the jury by its charm and by the informal residential character of its parts. While the administration of its living units would obviously be made difficult by their separation and distance from the main building, the jury felt that in this case and others where site and climate are favorable, such difficulty may be justified by the desire to provide smaller, more intimate, and even less institutional grouping of residents' rooms. The jury also recognizes that some efficiency and clarity of circulation in the central building was sacrificed in order to obtain such pleasant surroundings.

The jury debated longest on the checkerboard scheme proposed by the team of Katz, Waisman, Blumenkranz, Stein, and Weber of New York. It is a brilliant effort by talented designers. The serious objections raised by some members of the jury to the rigidity of this pattern may be met by the argument that by using the same size units throughout, prefabrication and great economy can be achieved. However, the general circulation to and through the units and the relationship between parts and functions are so adversely affected by this arbitrary scheme that the jury as a whole could not bring itself to give it more than a "mention." The jury must add that much of the fetching quality of this entry was obtained by the ingenious and spirited treatment of the various courts as living and recreational units.

Another scheme that merited the jury's attention was by the firm of Bellante & Clauss of Philadelphia with Hans Egli as designer. Its appeal lies in its economy of land, since all functions with the exception of the residence are condensed in a six-story building. Unfortunately, this virtue also occasioned its gravest fault—the splitting of the infirmary into two stories, an impossible solution from an economic and administrative point of view. The jury admired the composition of the units and the eloquence of the first-floor plan, but particularly of the residential wings, the layout of which expresses in a masterly way how a multiple living environment should be planned.

Finally, the jury selected for mention the scheme submitted by Norman H. Hoberman and John Gallagher, of Cambridge, Mass. It is the best of several schemes developed for a high-rise multistory building. The plan is compact and efficient and it has attempted the difficult task of providing a warm human environment in a tall building. The jury liked the scheme in spite of the confused and fragmented exterior composition.

The jury admired many other entries, the list of which would be too long for me to recite.

I will say in behalf of the jury that we were pleased with the results. We realize that much thinking has yet to be done on the problem, but we believe that these examples will serve as a stimulus and certainly as a starting point in our quest for the ideal solution to every problem that shall come to all of us for solution in the future.

FIRST PRIZE

Joe J. Jordan, Philadelphia
Hanford Yang, School of Architecture and Planning,
Massachusetts Institute of Technology

Comments by the contestants

The site: A relatively level plot in the northeast section of Philadelphia provides an area of more than 12 acres covered with fine trees and zoned for institutional use. To the north a well-established shopping center is still expanding, while the adjacent property to the south is being held for a new elementary school. It is recommended that the existing street between be closed. A recently dedicated city park borders the eastern property line, and across the street a middle-class residential area completes the fine list of neighbors.

The plan: The three residential units, arranged in a cluster about the main lounge area of the central building, provide intimate outdoor sitting spaces. Within the units, residents' rooms are grouped two and three together, creating pleasant circulation areas that lead to indoor facilities and the small communal gardens. The all-purpose room, chapel, shop, and library are closely related to the residents' rooms, so they should be well used. Beyond the open court lie the main entrance and the administrative suite. Service elements complete the north end of the central building. The glazed corridor connecting with the infirmary also serves as staff entrance.

The buildings: The exposed steel frame is sheathed with lightweight steel panels and plate glass. A 50-ft. module regulates the plan, with columns generally on 20-ft. centers. Natural light admitted through the clerestories dramatizes the administration and assembly areas. All space is air conditioned.

Comments by the architectural editor

This plan is a clear and direct expression of the functions the building is to perform, and fits within a clean, economical structure. The relationship between various areas and functions has been carefully studied, circulation is logical and direct, and obvious thought has everywhere been given to make this a pleasant place to live.

Common living facilities are located at the heart of the residential areas, and serve as a focal point for the home. The fact that all traffic to and from each residence unit passes through the main lounge will add to the sense of activity and interest. The residence units themselves are excellent examples of small-scale planning for a large-scale home. Each corridor is short, with at most nine rooms opening on it. Because the four corridors are offset about a central point, a resident can see only

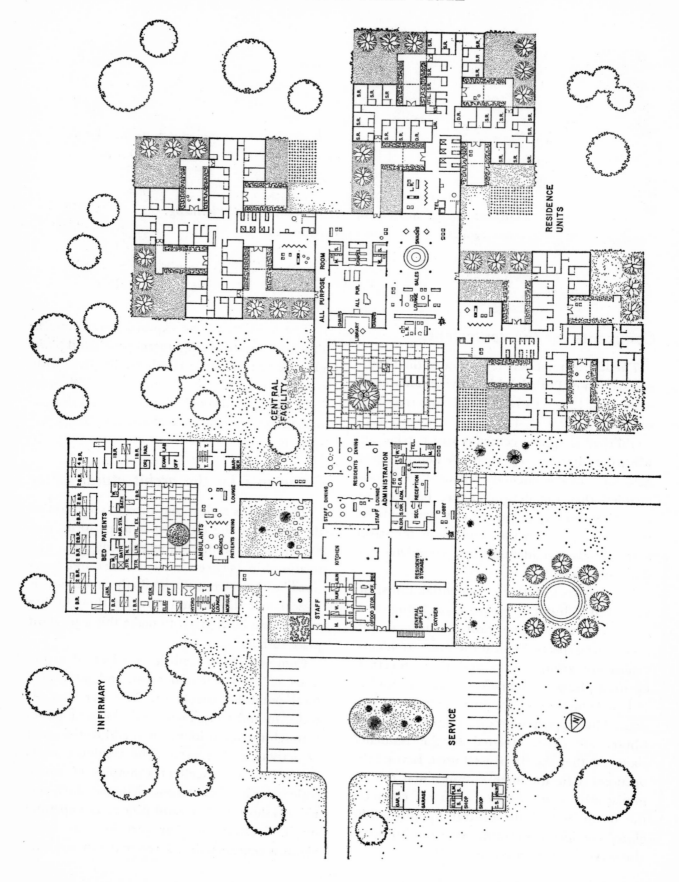

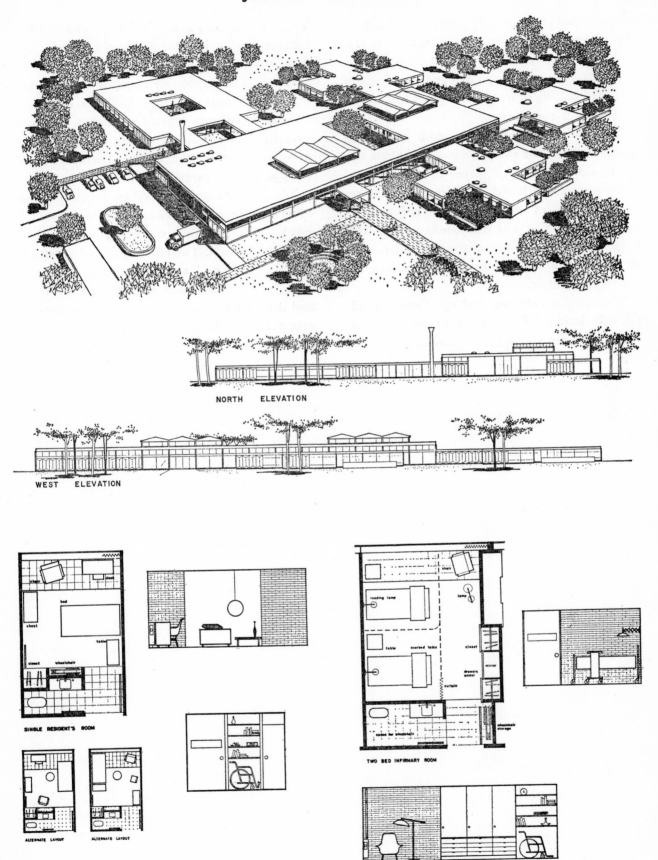

NORTH ELEVATION

WEST ELEVATION

SINGLE RESIDENT'S ROOM

ALTERNATE LAYOUT   ALTERNATE LAYOUT

TWO BED INFIRMARY ROOM

his own, and consequently a feeling of identity with the individual wing, rather than with the entire unit, is encouraged. Each wing has its own covered garden patio, and everywhere there is a feeling of freedom to go in and out at one's own pleasure.

The individual residence room is of adequate size, but the closet location prevents the use of a precious inside corner for furnishings.

Infirmary and health facilities are well related for services and visitors, but it is not desirable to have to pass through these facilities to get to the rooms. The central court lends an air of graciousness, but is otherwise somewhat difficult to justify.

The service entrance and functions are admirably isolated from all other parts of the home from the standpoint of vision and noise.

The kitchen feeds both the dining area and the infirmary from its central location. Residents' storage has good access.

It would be impossible to relate the administration area more directly to the main entrance.

This single-story scheme, though it encloses a relatively large volume, should be inexpensive to build because of the simple structural framework and clean exterior lines.

The exterior of the building articulates the difference in scale between the high central block, housing group activities, and the low residential wings. The effect is one of quietness and restraint, and as the building is viewed from both inside and out, breaks in the walls and the use of large amounts of glass affirm the easy relationship that exists between indoors and outdoors

SECOND PRIZE

Bellante & Clauss, Philadelphia
Jane West Clauss, Alfred Clauss

Comments by the contestants

The existing Brookwood Home for the Aged was selected for a rebuilding program. This 50-acre site is located within half a mile of the old suburban Philadelphia town of Media, with a population of 16,000, churches, shops, and an excellent medical clinic. It faces a beautiful housing development of the much publicized "Life Homes," which climb up and around the steep hillsides. The topography of the site itself, with a gentle slope down to the irregular water reservoir, lends itself to a cottage-type scheme.

For residential living, four units of three cottage wings each were provided. This plan maintains an economical supervision ratio of 20 residents to each nurse, while offering family life in a cottage designed for only 6 or 7 persons to the individual. The allocation of one cottage in each group to men reflects the ratio of the sexes, and encourages normal social relations in the living rooms grouped around the unit's solarium. To avoid corridor congestion, the bedrooms for wheelchair patients have been designed directly off living areas.

Cottages have been grouped around enclosed courtyards to emphasize the residential scale as well as to provide quiet landscaped areas where the inactive resident can relax on benches beside small pools, putter with flowers, or "gossip over the fence." All the cottages are set back from the road to take advantage of the excellent view of the woods and reservoir, and to place these within easy strolling distance for the nature lover and fisherman.

The central building houses the lounge, dining, and recreational areas, and the medical, administrative, and service facilities for the group. Thought has been given here to occupying the residents' leisure time. Arts and crafts rooms have been provided, and the nearby snack bar and shop has been designed to double in the evenings as a wine and beer bar, to be operated by a few of the more active group members.

A compact infirmary is located over the medical wing of the main building to utilize fully the same service facilities, kitchen, delivery, stores, lobby, and the like. From their elevated vantage point, the confined patients command an excellent view of both the natural surroundings and the activities of the remainder of the group.

The institution contains a total of 105 beds and 585,000 cu. ft. of space.

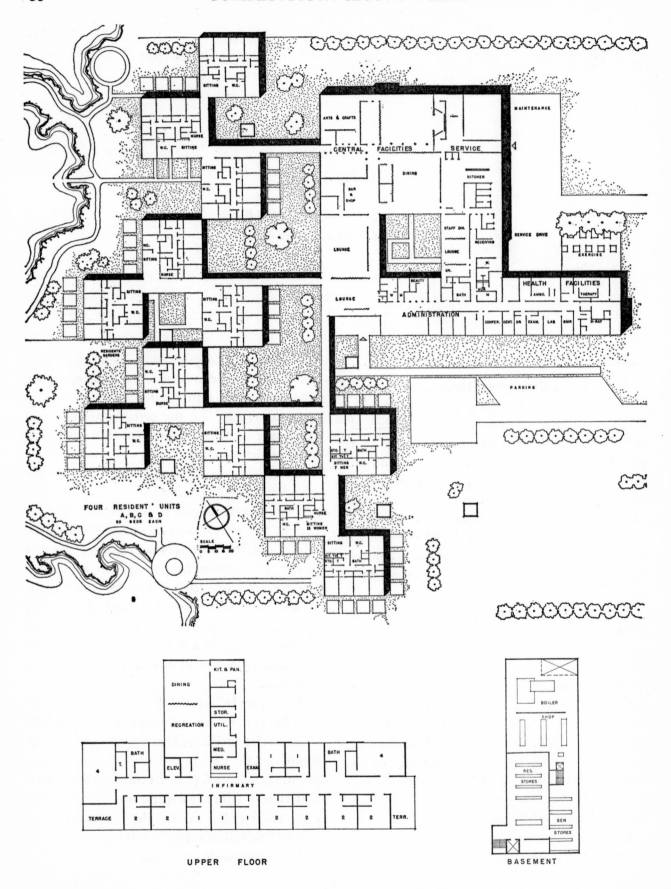

FOUR · RESIDENT · UNITS
A, B, C & D
20 BEDS EACH

SCALE
0   5   10   20

UPPER   FLOOR

BASEMENT

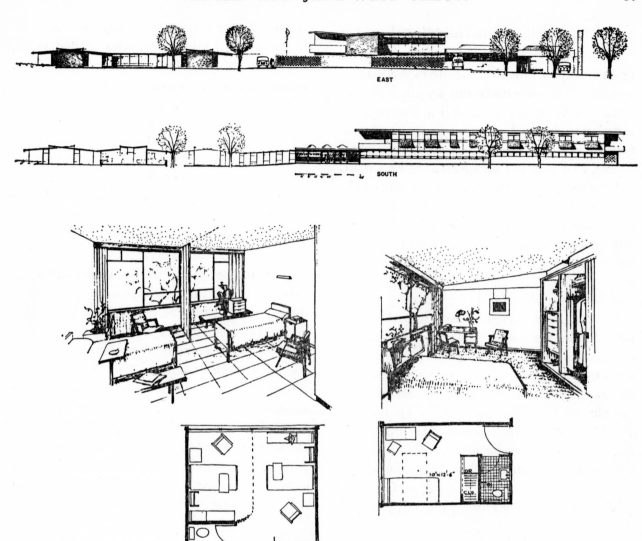

EAST

SOUTH

TYPICAL   INFIRMARY   AND   RESIDENCE   ROOM

Comments by the architectural editor

The residential scale of the residence units and the way in which they relate to the natural features of the site make this an unusually attractive scheme. There is also a directness of circulation from the central facilities to the residence units, each with three residence blocks, that may not be apparent at first sight.

Like the previous plan, residence units radiate from the central facilities, and traffic to and from these units circulates through the common lounge area. This in turn is divided into one large and two smaller seating areas with the private living room and snack bar centrally located—a very pleasant arrangement.

Dividing the residence units into three related blocks, the largest having seven residents, contributes to a sense of residential scale, and yet does not impede central nursing control in any important sense. However, the corridors are too narrow for wheelchair use, or for moving a resident by stretcher or bed. The individual rooms are also somewhat small, and freedom of furniture arrangement is limited by the loss of the main interior corner to closet access.

The residence unit lounges are well planned to provide for furniture arrangement in three or more small groups, all with garden views. This plan also provides a choice of outlook from residence rooms, ranging from intimate courts to the countryside.

The infirmary is well planned for nursing and has above-average lounging and terrace space; it is also well related to the ground floor health facilities and ambulance entrance. However, the feeling that infirmary residents should be out of sight or at least out of the main home is, unfortunately, reflected here.

The service facilities are well located, but appear to be unnecessarily complicated by placing storage and maintenance at the basement level. Within the building, staff facilities are well handled with a pleasant court outlook, but the employees should not have to use the receiving dock entrance. The alternative, of course, is for the employees to use the main entrance.

The exterior design has not received the same thoughtful development that the plan expresses, although what is shown indicates a scale and interest entirely consistent with the over-all scheme.

THIRD PRIZE

Gerhardt Liebmann, New York

Comments by the contestant

This home is designed for my home town—Medford, Oregon, a busy Western town situated in a rugged valley in southern Oregon. Specific regional climate problems are the hot western summer sun, controlled here by orientation, trellises, and trees; and the inclement winter weather for which the corridors are designed to double as foul-weather promenades.

The home is located in the East Civic Park of this growing town, whose industries are cattle, ranches, orchards, and lumber. The site is not overly large for maintenance (the municipal park crew is to be utilized) nor so small as to be crowded.

The quick growth of the town has jumbled residences and light and heavy commerce advantageously for the residents of the home. Hospitals, clinics, shops, theaters, and the like are within easy walking distance. The residential surroundings have influenced the design considerably. A community activities center is in the same park and offers opportunities for volunteer work. The park is much used by the townspeople, who will be in desirable contact with the residents.

The home is actively within the town, but has its own feeling of isolated independence, of being "ours." The isolation, yet sense of participation extends to the relationship between the infirmary and the residents, which is one of controlled togetherness. (Infirmary waiting room and patients' lounge are close to encourage visits.) Furthermore, patients have indoor access to the residents' chapel, and the like—visitors are controlled from the main office.

Regionalism is found in the patio retreat (oriented from the winter's worst), indigenous materials (such as sandstone), and in the use of heavy timber construction. This method of building is permitted in Medford's occupied buildings. The home uses a truss system with no loadbearing interior partitions. This offers easy conversion when requirements change, and yet it provides maximum sound control.

City participation is expressed in "open-arm" wings, and quiet isolation is physically expressed by the cloister-like patio.

Comments by the architectural editor

The design quality of this submission, so obvious at first from the exterior sketches and the presentation techniques of the plan, diminishes, at least to some extent, as the plan is examined in detail. If the winters are inclement, as the contestant states, why are residents forced

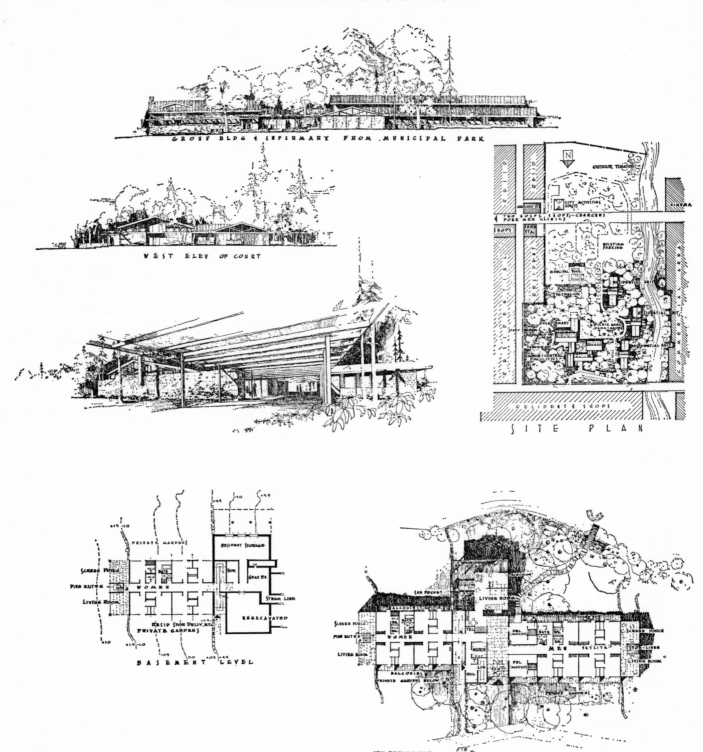

GROUP BLDG & INFIRMARY FROM MUNICIPAL PARK

WEST ELEV OF COURT

SITE PLAN

BASEMENT LEVEL

MAIN LEVEL & UPPER LEVEL (ONE-HALF FLIGHT)

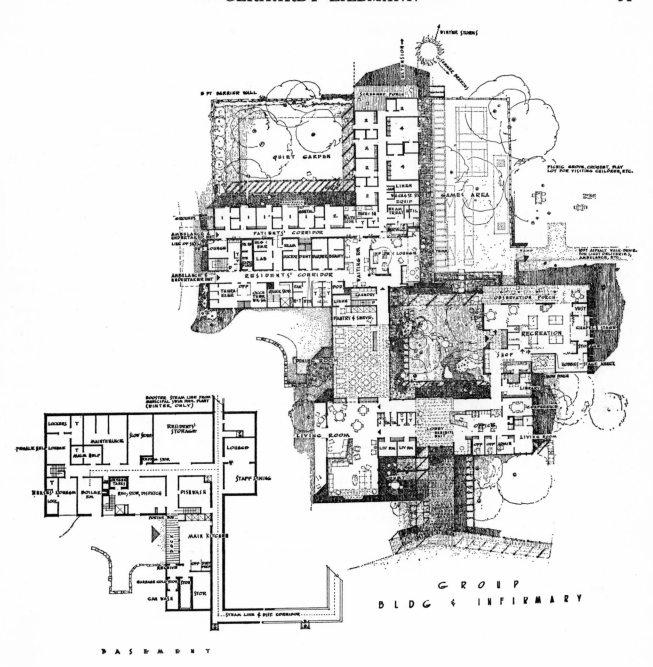

G R O U P
B L D G   &   I N F I R M A R Y

B A S E M E N T

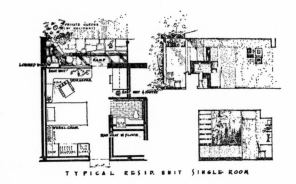

TYPICAL RESID. UNIT SINGLE ROOM

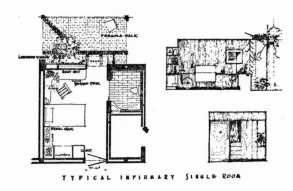

TYPICAL INFIRMARY SINGLE ROOM

to walk several hundred feet out-of-doors for each meal? The development of the property and placement of buildings has all the charm of a summer colony in the woods, but also all of the inconveniences.

The main lounge area provides beautiful space, but as a cul-de-sac is out of the main stream of activities. Residents coming to the main building circulate through the end of the infirmary, through the recreation room, or into the entrance lobby. This casualness or lack of direct circulation contrasts strongly with the other prize winners, but could be very pleasant in actual use.

The residence units themselves are split level plans, apparently to follow the slope of the land. In the event one of them were to be converted to nursing care, the nurses would have to use a ramp to care for two-thirds of their patients. At best, ramps are dangerous for the resident; these are impossibly steep. Here the hominess of ground hugging should have been surrendered to the practical problems of living in and operating a home for the aged.

Individual rooms again display the error of storage and its necessary access occupying the best corner in the room; as a consequence only one furniture layout is possible.

Such positive segregation by sex as is indicated here cannot be followed through in practice, and the necessity for flexibility would undoubtedly force some mingling. The alternative is to have the admission policy of the home dictated by the building layout.

The nursing center in the infirmary, although much too small, is admirably located for control of the corridors and lounge. Visitors' access is through the middle of the lounge or through the health waiting space, both rather confusing and unclear. Certainly, in this plan, the infirmary cannot be a neglected area.

Service elements are grouped in the basement with eight dumbwaiters and one elevator going up to the main floor for various reasons and at various points. Lack of understanding of the principles of the flow of supplies is manifested here. For instance, every dumbwaiter requires one person to load on one level and a second to unload on another level if the dumbwaiter is to be of any real use.

The employees are given leftover space for their lockers, lounges, and dining, all without daylight. The kitchen is about half the necessary size and gets its daylight through the loading dock. The service entrance is well located for everything but the dining room and lounge.

HONORABLE MENTION

Bellante & Clauss, Philadelphia
Hans G. Egli

Comments by the contestant

The proposed home for the aged is planned for an urban area of Philadelphia, adjacent to a large-scale housing development and over-looking the Schuylkill River with its busy boating activity and pleasant river drives. The purpose is to allow the inhabitants to grow old in a community of their own, but at the same time remain within the vicinity of their familiar outside surroundings.

The newcomer, who may possibly be reluctant to enter a "home," would be accommodated in the detached unit for newcomers, from which he can become acquainted with the other inhabitants and eventually move in with his new friends, choosing either to live in the apartment-type top floor of the main building, or to become a cottage dweller.

The infirmary (or rather the nursing unit), housed inconspicuously on the 3rd and 4th floors of the main building, can be expanded to the 5th and 6th floors if the number of those requiring nursing care should increase.

The object of the project is to provide for flexibility and varying requirements for the individual occupants. It is fitting that personal belongings and furnishings should be used in the occupant's private quarters. Thus, in a sense he remains a property owner, and the broom closet represents his independent way of life.

To prevent a vacuum in the oldsters' lives, the scheme provides for a purposeful way of living in which they can look after their friends' or relatives' children in their own neighborhood nursery, putter in the greenhouse, or sell their arts and crafts in the lounge shop. Basically, their home is a community within the community from which they come.

Comments by the architectural editor

This design provides three choices in resident accommodation: an independent apartment with kitchenette; a room in a single-story cottage for 13; and a room in a high-rise building. The plan has been evolved into a handsomely articulated building fitted easily on its site and taking every advantage of the view to the river.

The common facilities are grouped around the main lounge and entrance as are the residence units, and activity should be almost constant. It is, perhaps, unfortunate that the street is not visible from this point, as the river is, so that a choice of outlook could be available to the residents using the lounge. The multipur-

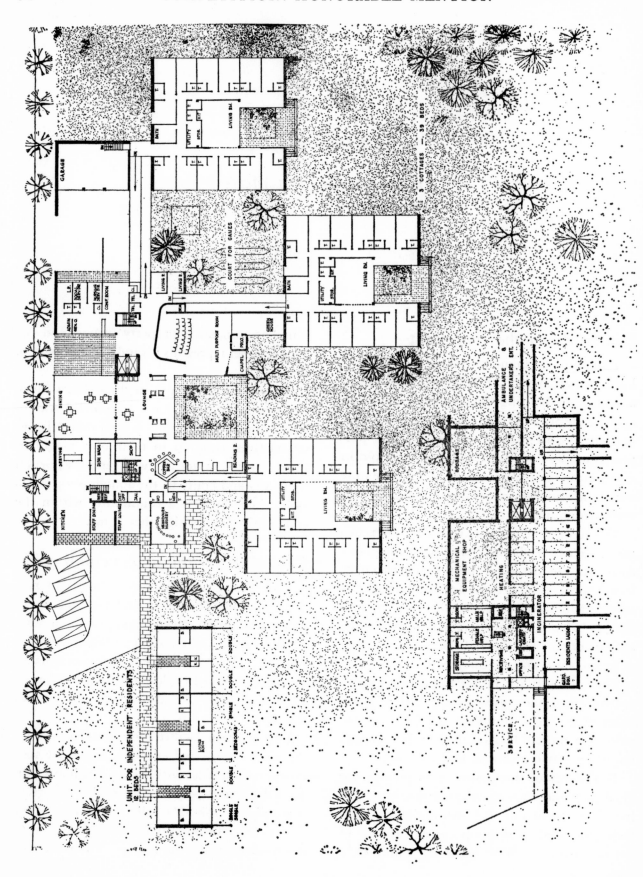

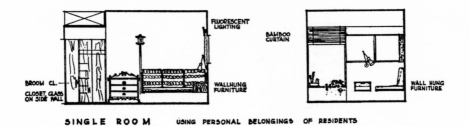

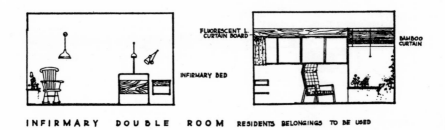

SINGLE ROOM   USING PERSONAL BELONGINGS OF RESIDENTS

INFIRMARY DOUBLE ROOM   RESIDENTS BELONGINGS TO BE USED

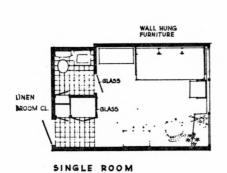

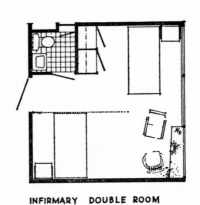

SINGLE ROOM

INFIRMARY DOUBLE ROOM

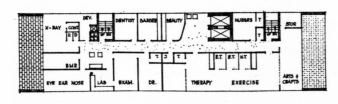

SECOND FLOOR
HEALTH MAINTENANCE
FACILITIES

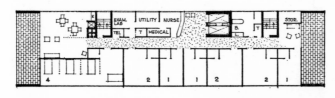

THIRD AND FOURTH FL.
INFIRMARY OR
        NURSING UNIT
26 BEDS

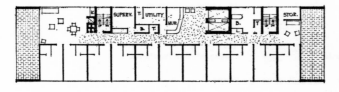

FIFTH AND SIXTH FLOOR
ELEVEN RESIDENTS UNITS
ALTERNATE USE:
        NURSING UNIT
22 BEDS

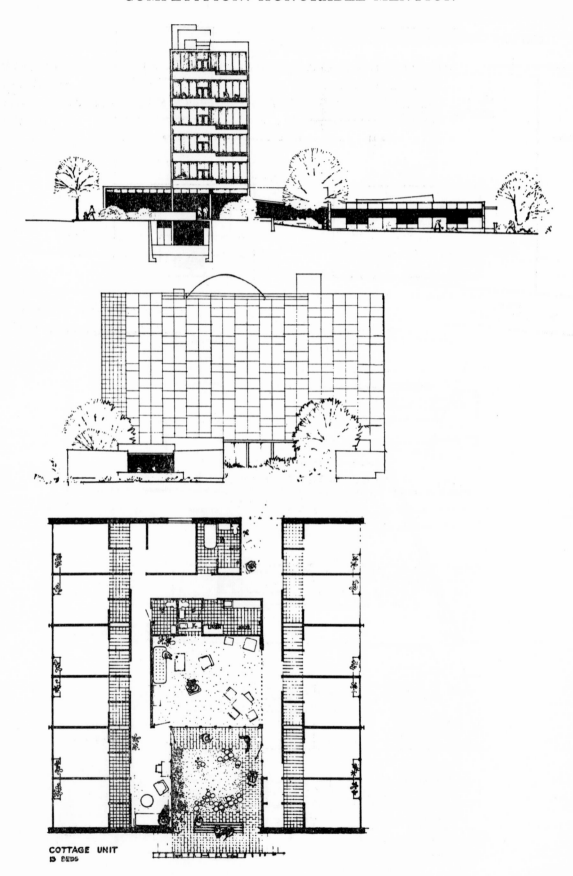

COTTAGE UNIT
13 BEDS

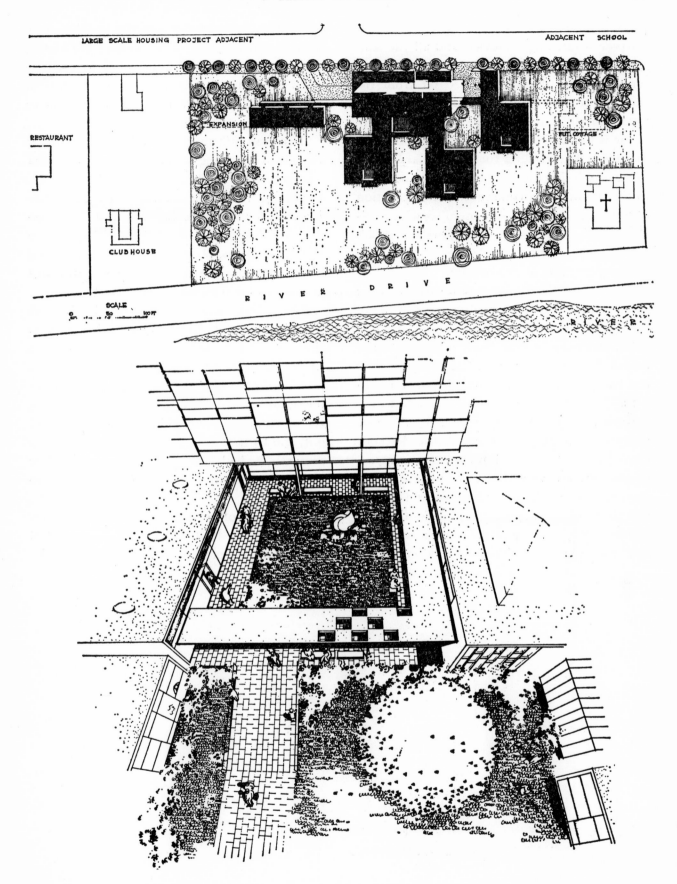

pose room seems to be planned for only one purpose—watching a movie—and all the seats would have to be turned around for a religious service. If the chapel is closed off from the multipurpose room, for the use of a few residents, it is difficult to get to. Access to the greenhouse is bad and a separate entrance should be provided. The reading room looks large for a home of this size, but of course it could be of use to the surrounding community. Incorporation of a nursery into the plan promises a very desirable neighborhood relationship, though administrators would no doubt need to give careful consideration to this feature.

The reason for the large ramp access to the residence cottages is not readily apparent. Like the third prize winner, the plan would be much more desirable on one level, if for no other reason than the fact that ramps form an effective barrier to anyone in a wheelchair trying to get about independently. They are also as exhausting as stairs to mount and, for those of uncertain footing, more dangerous to descend. Once inside a "cottage" however, the living arrangements are very pleasantly planned with their individual three-sided courts and with a maximum of six people on any corridor.

The individual self-contained apartments and rooms present interesting alternatives, while the rooms in the high-rise building provide a third choice of residence. Wall-hung furniture for the individual resident room is good for housekeeping, but denies freedom of furniture layout and requires an expensive structural supporting system.

The basic infirmary plan is good except for the lack of nursing supervision over the floor lounges. By dividing his infirmary on two levels, the designer has considerably increased operating costs for this important element. This burden will increase as the infirmary expands to the upper floors. Health facilities are well laid out, but the terrace at the left end of this unit appears to have no function.

The service elements are on two levels, with the kitchen, staff dining area, and lounge at the upper level, and are very well related to the other parts on that floor; but employees must enter via the loading dock in the basement, and their locker rooms have a confusing access. Residents' storage has been well worked out, and by use of the ramps, easy access to this area may be had from the residence units. The ambulance entrance seems to be impossible to get into.

The weak points in this plan seem to be outweighed by the fresh ideas it possesses as well as by its excellent scale and handsome facade.

HONORABLE MENTION

Norman L. Hoberman and John W. Gallagher;
Graduate School of Design, Harvard University

Comments by the contestants

In this home for the aged we have endeavored to provide an environment that would facilitate participation by the residents in the normal life of the community. To achieve this end, the home has been located within a residential area near the center of a large city. Across the street from the home is the Boston Public Garden, which in recent years has become a focus of community activity. Public transportation is nearby. Theaters, libraries, and other recreational facilities are close to the site. Churches and shops are within walking distance. Large medical centers are near.

Architecturally, the home looks outward over the city and the gardens so as to entice the residents with the surrounding life. A high-rise solution was dictated not only by the economics of the urban site, but also by the desire to maximize the spaces having the very desirable view of the gardens to the south.

Since the primary function of a home for the aged is residential, we have tried to minimize the institutional characteristics attendant upon a structure of this size. Thus, we have limited the number of residents per floor to thirteen. Balconies have been provided to maintain contact with the outside for people whose mobilty may be curtailed. A free fenestration has been used to avoid the sameness typical of institutional rooms. In any expansion of the home beyond the presently contemplated size, the residential scale would suffer; we have not, therefore, provided for it.

Several garages are available in the block to the northeast of the site which we feel would provide adequate parking.

Comments by the architectural editor

The necessity to build homes for the aged on limited urban sites will undoubtedly become a common problem. This design is very generously planned, having a volume almost double that of some of the other submissions. Generous space does not always result from multistory design.

Common facilities, such as the main lounge and dining area, are located on the tenth floor, probably for the view, but the lounge is reduced from the center of activities to an anteroom for dining. The multipurpose room one flight up opens onto a large roof terrace that should be popular.

Each of six resident floors provides for 13 residents—a small number from the standpoint

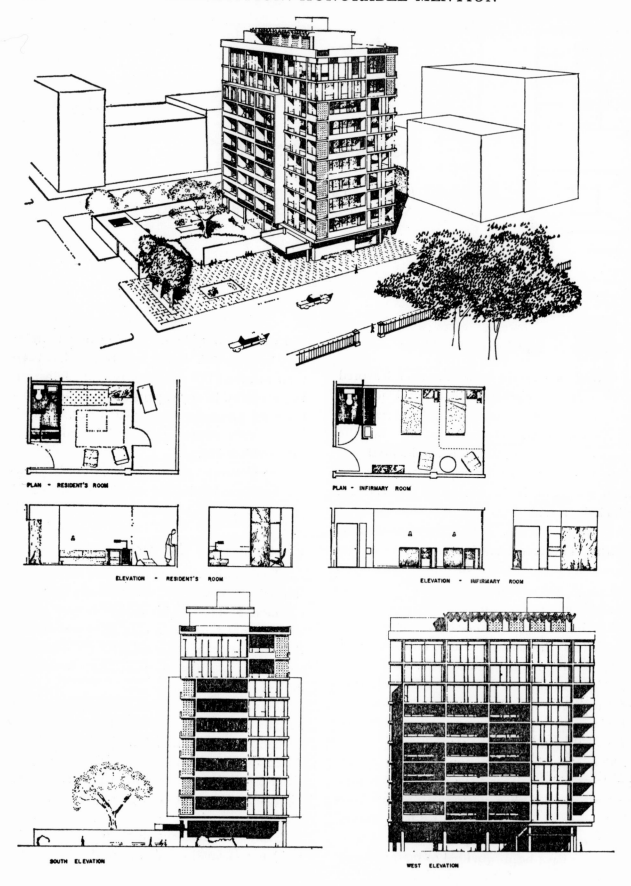

PLAN - RESIDENT'S ROOM

PLAN - INFIRMARY ROOM

ELEVATION - RESIDENT'S ROOM

ELEVATION - INFIRMARY ROOM

SOUTH ELEVATION

WEST ELEVATION

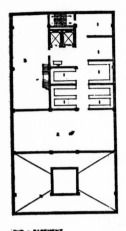

SUB - BASEMENT

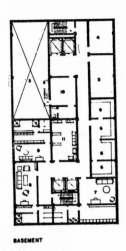

BASEMENT

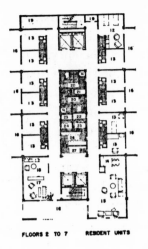

FLOORS 2 TO 7   RESIDENT UNITS

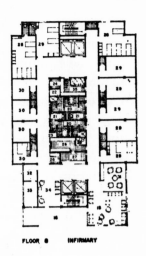

FLOOR 8   INFIRMARY

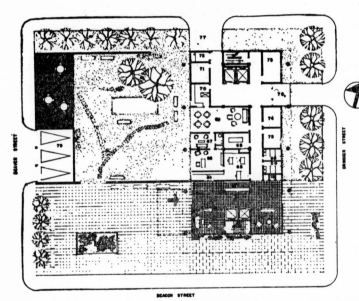

DEACON STREET

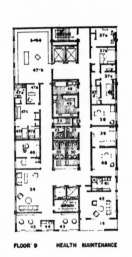

FLOOR 9   HEALTH MAINTENANCE

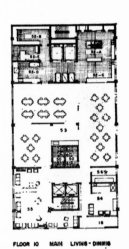

FLOOR 10   MAIN LIVING-DINING

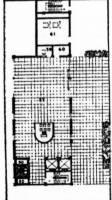

PENTHOUSE

1	General supply storage	
2	Residents' storage	
3	Boiler room	
4	Oxygen tank storage	
5	Ground maintenance storage	
6	Maintenance shops	
7	Male help lockers	
8	Nurses' lockers	
9	Female help lockers	
10	Janitor	
11	Laundry	
12	Double residence room	
13	Single residence room	
14	Kitchenette	
15	Living area	
16	Balcony	
17	Sitting space(s)	
18	Television area	
19	Residents' storage	
20	Bath and shower	
21	Toilet (wheelchair)	
22	Linen	
23	Janitor	
24	Equipment storage	
25	Staff toilet	
26	Utility	
27	Nurses' station	
28	Four-bed room	
29	Double room	
30	Private room	
31	Dining space	

32	Examination	
33	Treatment	
34	Waiting	
35	Diet kitchen	
36	Wheelchair and stretcher storage	
37	Radiographic suite	
a	Fluoroscopy	
b	Technician's office and files	
c	Radiography	
d	Dark room	
38	Eye, ear, nose and throat	
39	Examination room	
40	Doctor's office	
41	Doctors' lockers	
42	Doctors' lounge	
43	Barber	
44	Podiatrist	
45	Beauty shop	
46	Dentist	
47	Physical medicine suite	
a	Therapist's office	
b	Occupational therapy	
c	Exercise room	
d	Electrotherapy	
e	Hydrotherapy	
48	EKG and BMR	
49	Laboratory	
50	Toilet	
51	Reception desk	
52	Main kitchen	
a	Preparation	

b	Storage	
c	Serving	
d	Dishwashing	
e	Dietitian	
53	Main dining	
54	Library	
55	Main lounge	
56	Coffee shop	
57	Multipurpose room	
58	Chapel	
59	Projectionist	
60	Chair storage	
61	Mechanical equipment	
62	Lobby	
63	Small living room	
64	Information and switchboard	
65	General office	
66	Administrator's office	
67	Administrator's living room	
68	Conference	
69	Staff lounge and dining	
70	Food preparation	
71	Receiving and temporary storage	
72	Garbage storage and can washing	
73	Ambulance waiting	
74	Nursing service director	
75	Social service director	
76	Telephone	
77	Service entrance	
78	Ambulance entrance	
79	Garage	

of elevator service and, particularly, nursing. The double corridor plan locates the nursing, utility, and bathing facilities for efficiency, but does not seem to have shortened the visual length of the corridors. Provision for residents' storage on each floor is an excellent idea. The lounge areas are well planned if overly generous for thirteen people.

Separation of the two banks of elevators by the length of the building diminishes flexibility in use, and a confused resident could easily wander into the kitchen unless the elevators at the kitchen end of the building were limited to and keyed for service and stretcher use only. However, one elevator would be ample for this purpose. It is hoped that on the infirmary floor the nurses' station can be screened from the elevator lobby, so that the control aspect of the home will not seem dominant at one's arrival.

The infirmary and health maintenance floor plans are both good, but nursing would be easier in the infirmary if the nurses' station and utility room were located closer to the center of the group of patient rooms on the floor, rather than at one end.

Since the levels of all service facilities are different from that of service entrance, heavy elevator traffic becomes necessary. Furthermore, there can be no responsible control of the entrance. There will also be occasional conflict due to the dual function of the elevator lobby as service and ambulance entrance.

The exterior massing and design of the building is distinctly urban in character. Although the over-all effect is heavy, the facades are lively and broken, and one can imagine that the use of color might make this quite an attractive building.

HONORABLE MENTION

Architects Associated, New York
Sidney L. Katz, Taina Waisman, Joseph Blumenkranz, Richard G. Stein, Read Weber

Consultants:
Constantino Nivola, Jerome L. Strauss, Patrick S. Raspante, Ricardo Scofidio

Comments by the contestants

What makes this a home?
> a residential scale for the units
> a feeling of a little village with avenues and lanes
> a profusion of garden courts
> a room that becomes an individual apartment opening on its own terrace
> the opportunity to be alone or in various groups
> no cell-flanked, funnel-like corridors
> a main street lined with shops and gardens, with benches and social rooms
> a snack bar and dining room
> a variety of terraces—some with fountains, some with birds, some with waist-high gardening patches, some with game tables or orchards or pools
> an avoidance of the awesome, of overpowering institutional scale

What makes this a home for the aged?
> a simple, direct circulation in which street names and identifying color unobtrusively guide the residents
> an absence of ramps or stairs
> elimination of doors wherever possible

> security from fire through direct access to outdoors and fireproof construction
> gardens designed for activities of older people
> cross ventilation in all rooms for comfort and to dissipate odors

What makes this a home for the aged of a community?
> location as part of a total area development
> contiguity to facilities for the elderly and to a community center in a large urban housing project
> full integration into the life of the neighborhood

How is it built?
> a repetitive concrete ribbed shell on corner columns
> reusable forms and lift-slab process for economy of construction
> a cellular pattern for ease of expandability by the addition of component units

Comments by the architectural editor

This design, with its main street and connecting lanes, forms a little village of alternating buildings and courts that would be an ex-

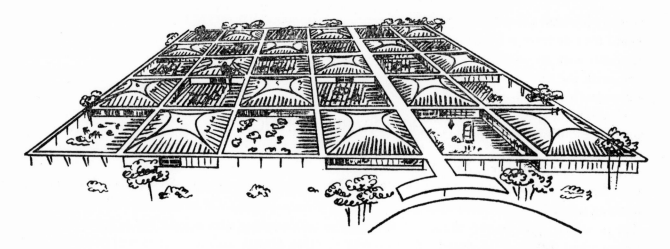

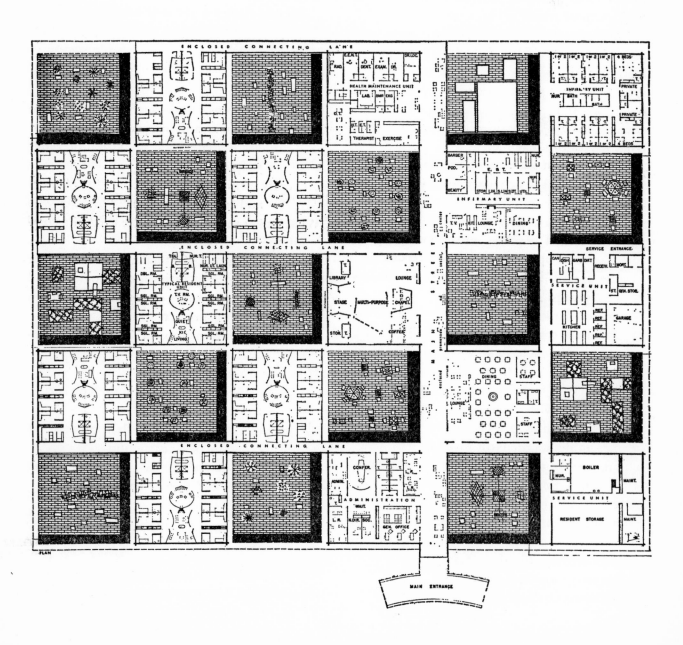

tremely pleasant place to live in. The checker-board tour de force is imposed on the required elements with an unexpected degree of success and, with the exception of one or two failures, represents a brilliant piece of planning.

Common facilities center around the multi-purpose room with the main lounge next to the dining area. Small sitting groups are located all along the main street, which, although more than 300 ft. long, is broken by walls of glass opening upon five courtyards alternately, from side to side. Access to the chapel is easy and independent when it is closed off from the multipurpose room.

Residence units are small in scale and planned for pleasant living. A strong sense of identity with one's own living unit could easily arise here, in much the same way that one's home on a street stands apart from others. The circulation pattern is direct, although the access lanes are overly long.

Individual rooms appear small, cluttered, and relatively rigid because so much is built in. The subcorridor into the room is too narrow, and the use of folding doors is questionable, particularly at the toilet, where stacking is at the least convenient location. Again, a very useful interior corner is sacrificed. With such a generous use of space throughout the remainder of the home, the rooms appear out of character.

The infirmary plan simply does not fit into the typical structural unit. By locating the nurse and particularly her utility rooms outside the unit, a nearly perfect plan fails. The necessity to make the utility rooms too large simply to fill up the second infirmary unit reveals the fallacy of attempting such an approach to planning with a building as complicated as this. Health maintenance is well planned.

Service elements are well related to the balance of the building, but again, because of the structural module, two service entrances are required. Kitchen service to the infirmary as well as to the dining room is easy and direct. Staff facilities are well conceived and should be conducive to high employee morale.

It would be very interesting to see this plan developed further, perhaps to the point where no compromises would have to be forced on it by such a powerful architectural concept. In such an event, this building would become an example of first rank architecture.

Appendix A: Population Data

U.S. population 65 and over in quasi-households

	1950	1980
In quasi-households	701,785	1,403,570
institutions	385,419	770,838
other	316,366	632,732

NOTE: Figures for 1950 are from Henry D. Sheldon's *The Older Population of the United States,* John Wiley & Sons, New York (1958), p. 202. Figures for 1980 are based on U.S. Bureau of the Census population projections, 1950–1980; the assumption is made that the predicted doubling of the total population aged 65 and over would result in a similar doubling of population aged 65 and over in institutions and other quasi-households.

U.S. population 65 and over

Year	Population, millions
1950	12.3
1955	14.1
1960	15.8
1965	17.6
1970	19.5
1975	21.9
1980	24.5

SOURCE: U.S. Bureau of the Census, Current Population Reports, Series P–25, No. 187, November 10, 1958, p. 17

Marital status of U.S. population 65 and over
As of March, 1957, in thousands

	Men			Women		
	Total	65–74	75 & over	Total	65–74	75 & over
Total	6,754	4,576	2,178	7,927	5,118	2,809
Single	496	347	149	636	395	241
Married	4,622	3,450	1,172	2,890	2,292	598
spouse present	4,428	3,314	1,114	2,753	2,184	569
spouse absent	194	136	58	137	108	29
separated	83	62	21	43	34	9
other	111	74	37	94	74	20
Widowed	1,516	689	827	4,307	2,351	1,956
Divorced	120	90	30	94	80	14

SOURCE: U.S. Bureau of the Census, Current Population Reports, Series P–20, No. 81, March 19, 1958, p. 8

Income of persons 65 and over

By marital status and sex (1956 civilian, noninstitutional, nonfarm population of the U.S.)

	Total	Single	Married	Widowed or Divorced
Men				
Number	5,558,000	358,000	3,842,000	1,358,000
Per cent	100.0	100.0	100.0	100.0
with income	94.6	91.3	96.8	89.0
without income	5.4	8.7	3.2	11.0
Per cent of those with income	100.0	100.0	100.0	100.0
$1–$1,999	62.0	77.1	56.0	76.9
$2,000–$3,999	22.2	17.3	24.8	15.7
$4,000–$5,999	9.9	3.9	11.9	5.1
$6,000 and over	5.8	1.7	7.3	2.3
Women				
Number	6,887,000	550,000	2,420,000	3,917,000
Per cent	100.0	100.0	100.0	100.0
with income	72.3	84.1	59.4	78.9
without income	27.7	15.9	40.6	21.1
Per cent of those with income	100.0	100.0	100.0	100.0
$1–$1,999	90.0	72.2	96.1	89.6
$2,000–$3,999	7.4	19.2	2.9	7.9
$4,000–$5,999	1.7	5.0	0.7	1.7
$6,000 and over	0.9	3.6	0.3	0.8

SOURCE: U.S. Bureau of the Census, Current Population Reports, Series P–20, No. 81, March 19, 1958, p. 12

Appendix B: Building Costs

No cost figures were required of contestants in the competition and no limitations were placed on expenditures. Therefore, no estimate of the cost of construction of the prize-winning designs can be given. The following remarks are appended only to provide some idea of the costs involved for the benefit of groups without experience in financing buildings of this type.

Many variables affect costs, and it has been estimated that more than a thousand cost decisions must be made during the course of a building project.

An informal inquiry by the National Committee on the Aging in 1957 revealed that the cost of building a home for the aged with infirmary facilities ranged from $8,000 to $12,000 per bed.

One home under construction in New York State in 1958 meets, to some extent, the competition specifications. This home provides for 80 single rooms (some with private bath), 10 two-room suites with kitchenette and bath, and a 20-bed infirmary with one four-bed, six double, and four single rooms. Also included are physicians' examining rooms, a chapel, recreation room, large lounge, three small lounges, dining room, solarium, and a gift shop. The cost, excluding land, architects' fees, legal fees, and movable equipment and furnishings, was estimated to be $1,600,000, or about $13,000 per bed.

The following opinion was expressed by Mr. Harold Lund, a consultant on services to the aged, at the Southwestern Regional Conference on Aging held under the auspices of the National Committee on the Aging in Houston, Texas, on October 20, 1958:

"It can be assumed that an adequate physical plant in a desirable location will be expensive. An article in the Social Security Bulletin (May 1958) reports recent costs ranging from $3,000 to $14,000 per bed in nursing homes widely spread over the country and subject to a variety of state requirements. A modern building erected by a church organization in Hartford, Connecticut in 1955 cost $6,000 per bed for construction alone, and $9,000 including equipment. This home was planned so that the normal capacity of 150 can be increased to 225 by adding a bed in rooms that are suitably large. This expansion would reduce average cost per bed to $6,000.

"The average cost of 125 nursing homes receiving grants through the Hill-Burton program of hospital and medical facilities construction through June of this year was $11,000 per bed. Of these homes, 70 were under voluntary auspices and 46 were public. The average capacity was 47 beds. Although costs will vary in different communities, it is interesting to note that they are frequently similar in widely separated places.

"From these data it appears that it would be unwise to assume that a building could be provided for less than $10,000 per bed, including furnishings, an initial inventory of supplies, and reserve for use in maintenance until full occupancy and operating income could be attained."

The above figures are not intended to be definitive. Construction cost estimates should be the basis for planning any building project. Only the architect can prepare such estimates with any degree of accuracy. It is possible to secure the services of an architect, for a reasonable fee, for this preliminary budgeting phase without any further commitment. It can be understood at the outset that such a consulting architect may compete with others for the total job when the time comes for final selection of an architect.

It is not generally considered good ethical practice for an architect to offer these preliminary services free in the hope of getting the job. The planning group will, however, find the payment of a modest fee for the budgeting phase a good investment if they wish to postpone selection of an architect until some basic decisions about the building have been made.

Appendix C: Bibliography

The Architect Looks at Housing the Aged. Housing Research Council of Southern California, Inc., Pasadena (1953).

Aronson, Morton. "Psychiatric Management of Disturbed Behavior in a Home for the Aged," *Geriatrics,* January 1956, pp. 39–43.

Bream, C. C. "Recreation and Education as Therapy for the Aged." In *Services for the Aging.* (University of Florida, Institute of Gerontology). University of Florida Press, Gainesville (1957).

"Buildings for the Aged," *Architectural Record,* September 1954, pp. 185–208.

"Buildings for the Aging," *Architectural Record,* May 1956, pp. 196–226.

Charter for the Aging. New York State Conference on Problems of the Aging at Albany, New York (1955).

Directory of State Agencies Having Primary Legal Responsibility for Standards of Maintenance and Operation of Hospitals, Nursing Homes, Homes for the Aged, and Other Similar Facilities Except Those Operated by Federal and State Governments. U.S. Public Health Service, Division of Hospital and Medical Facilities, Washington, D.C. (1956).

Dobrin, Leo. "Rehabilitation in Institutional Geriatrics: a Preliminary Report," *New York State Journal of Medicine,* January 1952, pp. 81–85.

Donahue, Wilma, *ed. Housing the Aging: Report of the University of Michigan Fifth Annual Conference on Aging, Ann Arbor, July 24–26, 1952.* University of Michigan Press, Ann Arbor (1954).

"Environmental Needs of the Aging: Symposium," *Geriatrics,* April 1957.

Food Problems in Homes for the Aged. Community Council of Greater New York, New York (1955).

For the Aged. (Special [October 1958] issue of the *Journal of Housing*), National Association of Housing and Redevelopment Officials, Chicago (1958).

Frazier, Mrs. Loudell, and Gebhart, Dorothy L. *The Community and Institutions for the Aged.* American Public Welfare Association, Chicago (n.d.).

Goldfarb, Alvin I. "Psychotherapy with Aged Persons: Pattern of Adjustment in a Home for the Aged," *Mental Hygiene,* October 1955, pp. 608–621.

Goldmann, Franz, and Deardorff, Neva. *Organization of Personal Health Services in Homes for the Aged.* Council of Jewish Federations and Welfare Funds, Inc., New York (1958).

Guide for Intake in Homes for the Aged. Community Council of Greater New York, New York (1953).

Guidebook for Organization and Management of Nursing Homes and Homes for the Aging. Kansas State Department of Social Welfare, Topeka (1955).

Health Guide for Institutions Serving Older People. Philadelphia Health and Welfare

Council, Inc., Division on Aging, Philadelphia (1958).

Herz, Kurt G. and Zelditch, Morris, *ed. Administration of Homes for the Aged: Selected Papers on Management and Program Planning.* Council of Jewish Federations and Welfare Funds, Inc., New York (n.d.).

A Home in the Later Years. New York State Association of Councils and Chests, New York (1953).

Homes for the Aged: a Study of Developments During the Past Ten Years. Community Council of Greater New York, New York (1955).

Housing an Aging Population: a Contribution of the Subcommittee on Standards for Housing the Aged and Infirm. American Health Association, Committee on the Hygiene of Housing, New York (1953).

Housing for the Elderly: a Report of the Industry Advisory Committee. U.S. Federal Housing Administration, Washington, D.C. (1957).

The Impact of Changing Times on Homes for the Aged. A two-day conference of board staff members of homes for the aged in Illinois, March 12–13, 1957. Chicago (1957).

Kleemeier, Robert W. "An Analysis of the Counseling Function in Homes for the Aged." In *Services for the Aging.* (University of Florida, Institute of Gerontology). University of Florida Press, Gainesville (1957).

———— "An Analysis of Group Living for Older People." In *Aging: A Current Appraisal.* (University of Florida, Institute of Gerontology). University of Florida Press, Gainesville (1957).

Kostick, Abraham, and Rosen, Theodore. *Extension Program of a Regional Home for the Aged: an Aspect of Community Planning with and for Small Communities.* (1958).

Lakin, Martin, and Dray, Melvin. "Psychological Aspects of Activity for the Aged," *The American Journal of Occupational Therapy,* July-August 1958, Part I.

Manual for Board Members: a Guide to the Functions of the Home and the Responsibilities of the Board Membership. Drexel Home, Inc., Chicago (1954).

A Manual for the Nursing Procedures in Use at Drexel Home. Drexel Home, Inc., Chicago (n.d.).

Manual of Policies and Procedures. Pacific Home, California (1957).

A Manual of Policies and Procedures: Institutions for Aged Persons. California State Department of Social Welfare, Sacramento (1956).

Manual for Volunteers. Drexel Home, Inc., Chicago (1958).

National Conference on Nursing Homes and Homes for the Aged, February 25–28, 1958, Washington, D.C. U.S. Public Health Service, Washington, D.C. (Public Health Service Publication No. 625). (1958).

Nicholson, Edna. *Planning New Institutional Facilities for Long-Term Care.* G. P. Putnam's Sons, New York (1956).

A Psychiatric Approach to Institutional Work with the Aged. Community Service Society of New York, New York (1955).

Rosen, Theodore, and Kostick, Abraham. "Separation and Adjustment Problems in a Home for the Aged," *Social Work,* January 1957, pp. 36–40.

The Small Home for the Aged: Cost and Staffing. Council of Jewish Federations and Welfare Funds, Inc., New York (1956).

Shore, Herbert. "Group-Work Programs in Homes for the Aged," *Social Service Review,* June 1952, pp. 181–194.

Standards of Care for Older People in Institutions. National Social Welfare Assembly, Inc., National Committee on the Aging, New York (1953, 1954).

Section I: *Suggested Standards for*

Homes for the Aged and Nursing Homes.

Section II: *Methods of Establishing and Maintaining Standards in Homes for the Aged and Nursing Homes.*

Section III: *Bridging the Gap Between Existing Practices and Desirable Goals in Homes for the Aged and Nursing Homes.*

Standards of Design: Housing the Elderly. Massachusetts State Housing Board, Boston (1954).

Toward Independent Living for Older People: a Report on Housing and Community Services. Philadelphia Housing Association, Committee on Housing for Older People, Philadelphia (1958).

Williams, Ralph C. *Nursing Home Management.* F. W. Dodge Corporation, New York (1959).

Zelditch, Morris. *The Home for the Aged: an Address Before the New England Regional Meeting of Homes for the Jewish Aged, April 28, 1957.*

Index